Guitar Thesaurus
Vol.II Advanced Scales
by Stefanos Nikas

"It does not matter how slowly you go as long as you do not stop."

*I would like to give special thanks to **Tasos Asonitis**
for the help he provided me.*

Cover Photo by Stefanos Nikas

First Edition

ISBN: 978-1-304-70234-0

All diagrams created using

Table Of Contents

Introduction

Just a few days after "Guitar Thesaurus: The Complete Guide to Scales, Chords, Arpeggios" was published I remember myself going through the pages looking at the scales included in it. It was only then, when it crossed my mind for the first time:

"Every widely used scale was there, but what about all those strange, exotic, traditional scales that are used in different kinds of music worldwide, such as ethnic music? These scales are not so often used on guitar but what if someone could gather the most of them in a book that would particularly address to the guitarists' community?"

A few suggestions made by fellow guitarists and friends provoked the idea that "Guitar Thesaurus" must have a sequel! So, here is "Guitar Thesaurus Vol.II: Advanced Scales". In Vol.II, all the aforementioned scales that were not a part of Vol.I, are included: Harmonic Major, Neapolitan and Hungarian families and their respective modes, Japanese, Oriental, Enigmatic, Bebop scales, you name it. Some of these scales were mapped out on a guitar fretboard for the very first time! More than 60 new scales, some which you will not be able to find anywhere else.

Following the steps of Vol.I, I have categorized the scales according to the "family" they belong to. I begin with the Harmonic Major scale and then all the modes of it, Dorian b5, Phrygian b4 etc. In the same way, I present the Neapolitan Major and Neapolitan Minor followed by their respective modes, in scale degree order. For example, the mode that follows Neapolitan Minor, is Lydian #6 because it starts from the second degree of it. Then goes Dominant Augmented, the one that starts from the third degree, and so on.

So, why the term "Advanced"? Some of these scales do have tricky fingerings because they were developed for traditional instruments, not for the guitar. However, the reason I call these scales "Advanced" is that they are used by guitar players that have already built their scale vocabulary and want to expand their musicianship to the next level.This could be achieved by incorporating sounds and textures that are not so common to the biggest part of the world. I believe that this book helps the advanced guitarist to create what we perceive as "personal touch".

Vol.II has also a bonus section for all of you crazy string burners out there. This section includes the scales mentioned in Vol.I (Major, Harmonic Minor and Melodic Minor families along with their respective modes) in 3-note-per-string pattern. This way you can practice your technique very efficiently and at the same time improve your scale vocabulary.

"Guitar Thesaurus Vol.I" gives you what you need in order to play anything you comes across. "Guitar Thesaurus Vol.II" takes it a step beyond by helping the advanced player to create a distinct and personal sound. Be unique, be yourself.

Stefanos Nikas

Reading Diagrams

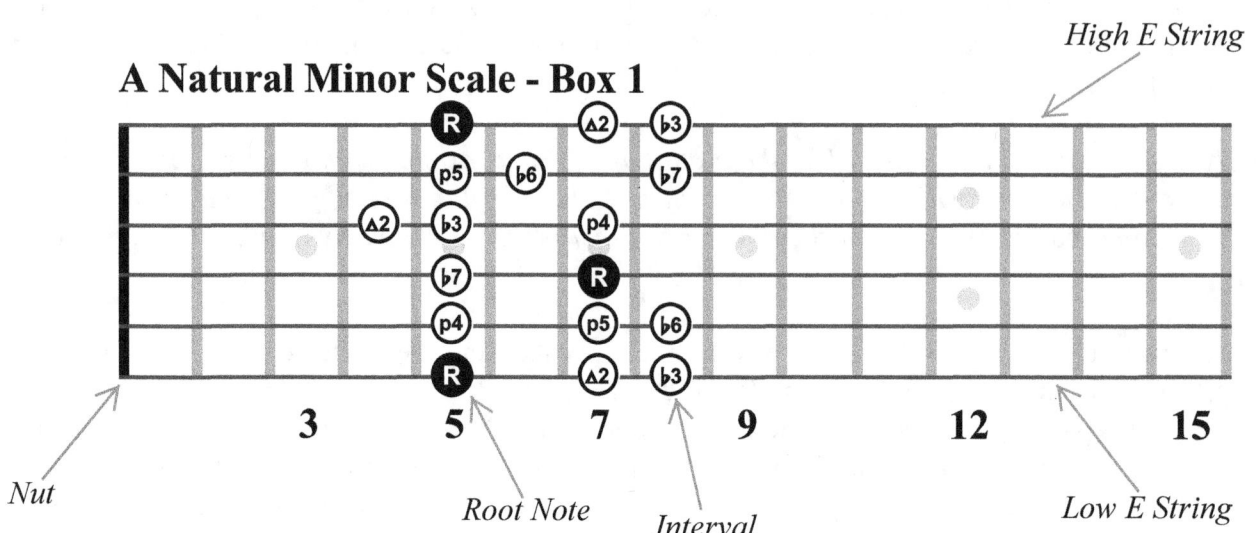

A Natural Minor Scale - Box 1

High E String

Nut

3   5   7   9   12   15

Root Note

Interval

Low E String

<u>Notes</u>

R	=	Root
b2	=	Minor 2nd
Δ2	=	Major 2nd
bb3	=	Diminished 3rd
b3	=	Minor 3rd
Δ3	=	Major 3rd
b4	=	Diminished 4th
p4	=	Perfect 4th
b5	=	Diminished 5th
p5	=	Perfect 5th
bb6	=	Diminished 6th
b6	=	Minor 6th
Δ6	=	Major 6th
bb7	=	Diminished 7th
b7	=	Minor 7th
Δ7	=	Major 7th

"All shapes are movable. They can be played anywhere on the fretboard depending on what key you are playing in."

A Harmonic Major Scale

Box 1

Box 2

Box 3

Box 4

Box 5

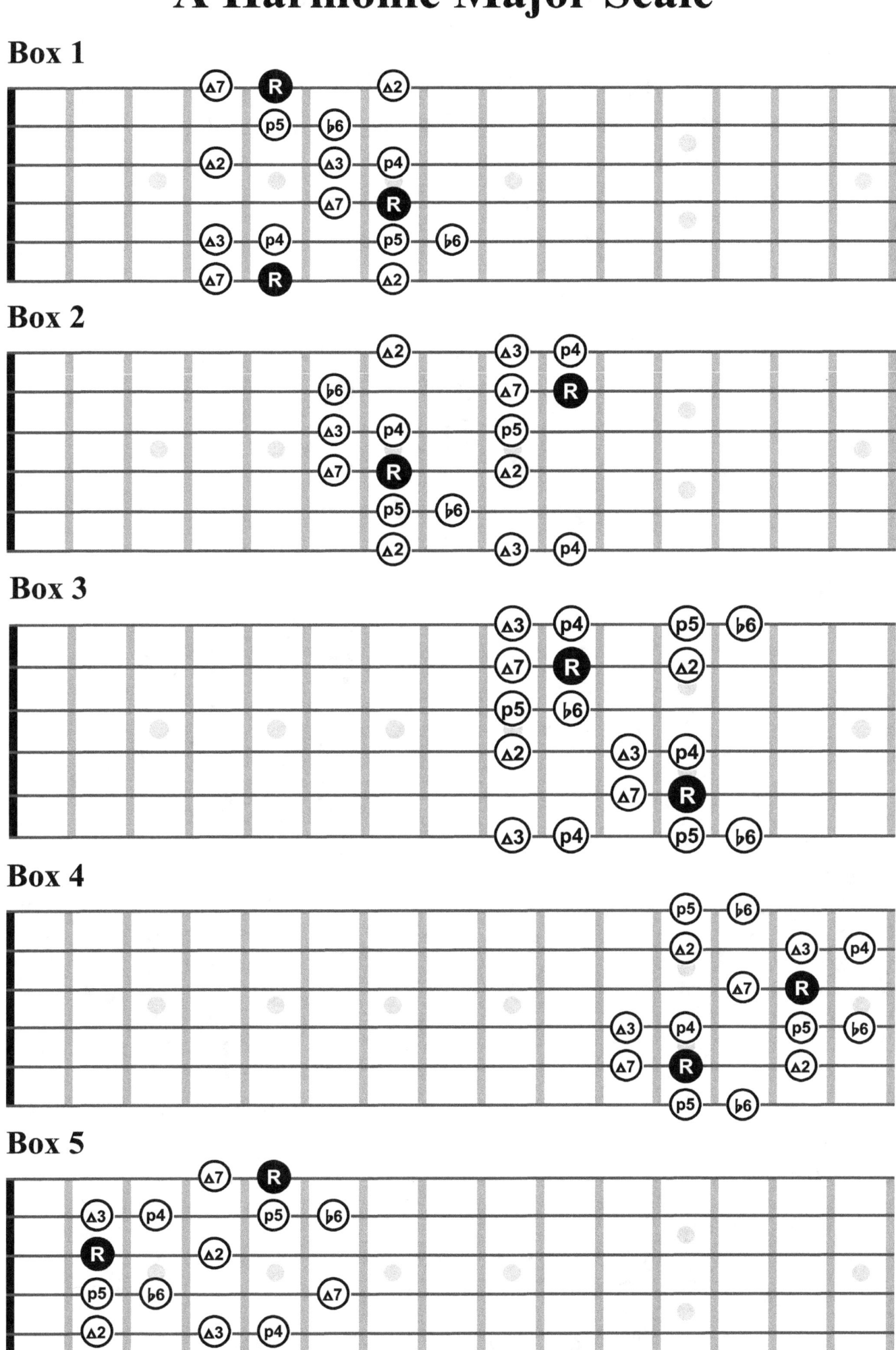

A Dorian b5 Scale

Box 1

Box 2

Box 3

Box 4

Box 5

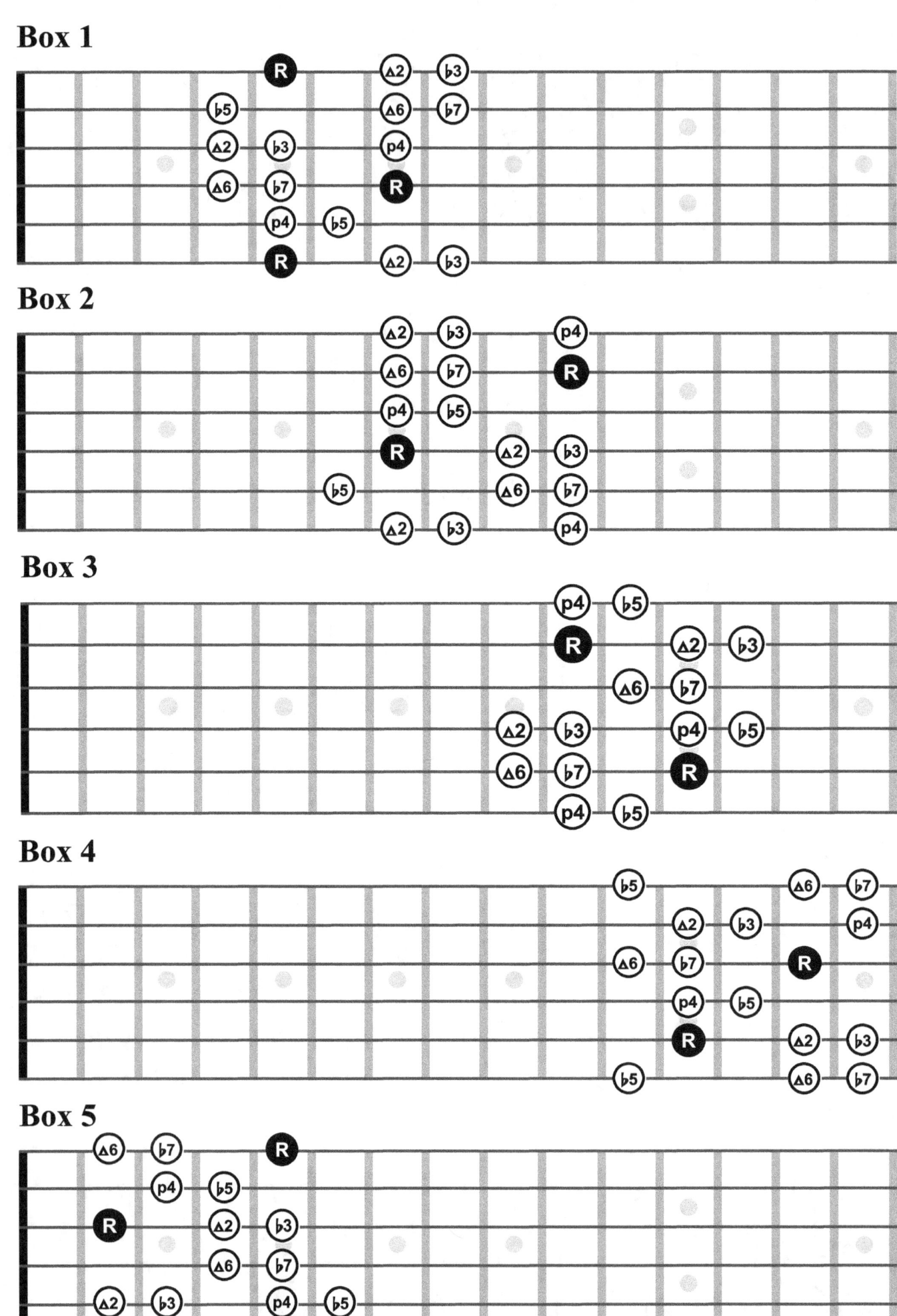

A Phrygian b4 Scale

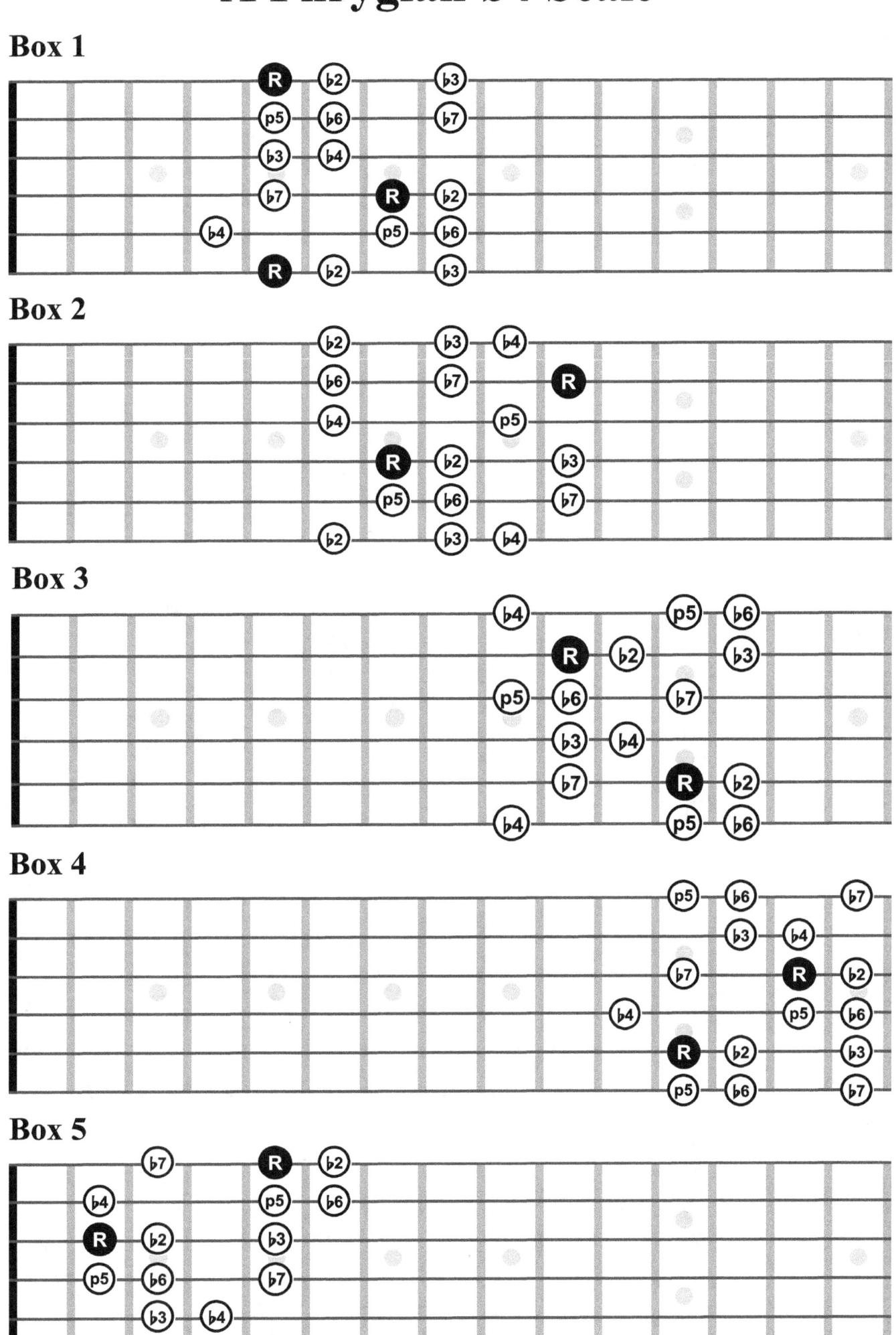

A Lydian b3 Scale

Box 1

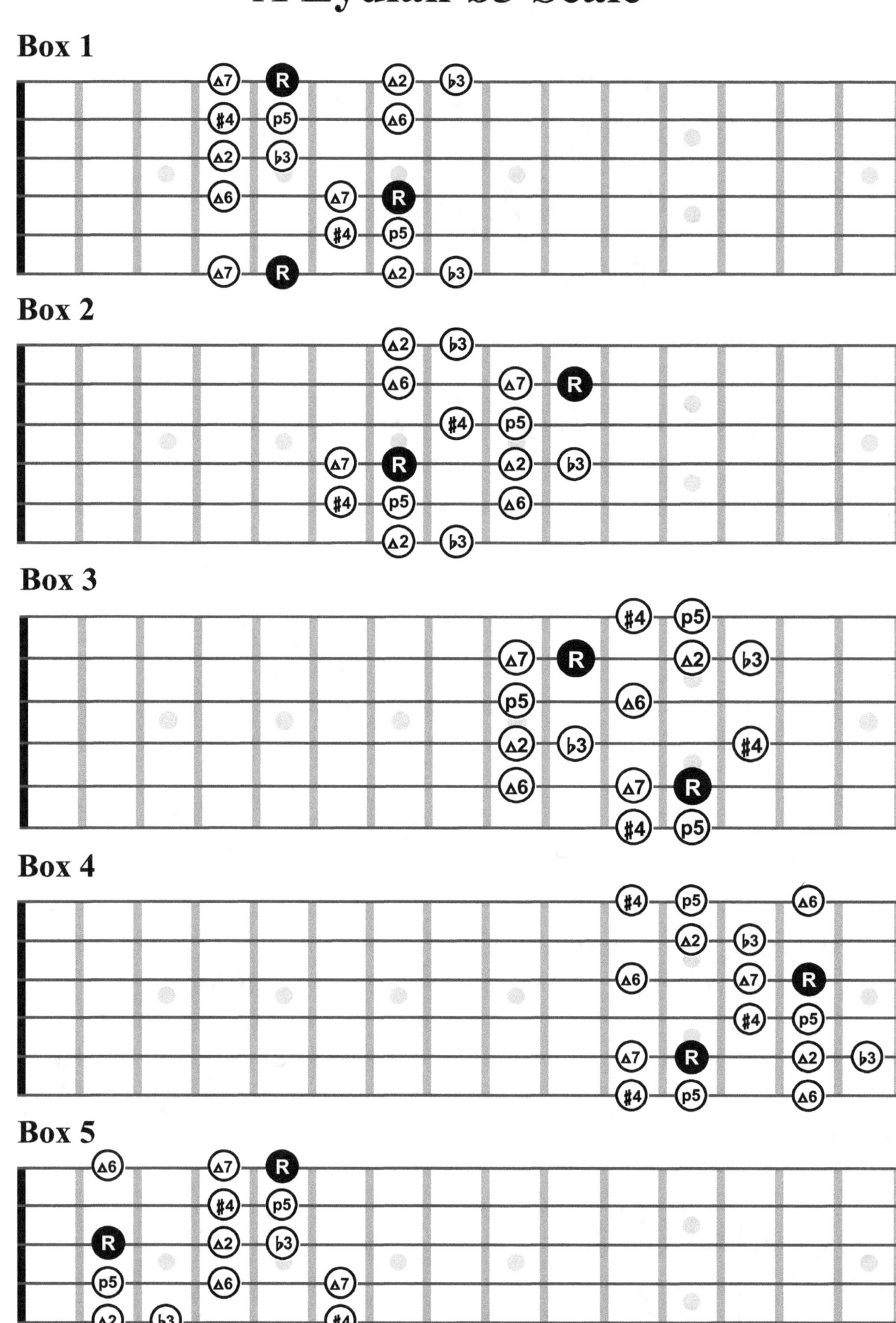

Box 2

Box 3

Box 4

Box 5

A Mixolydian b2 Scale

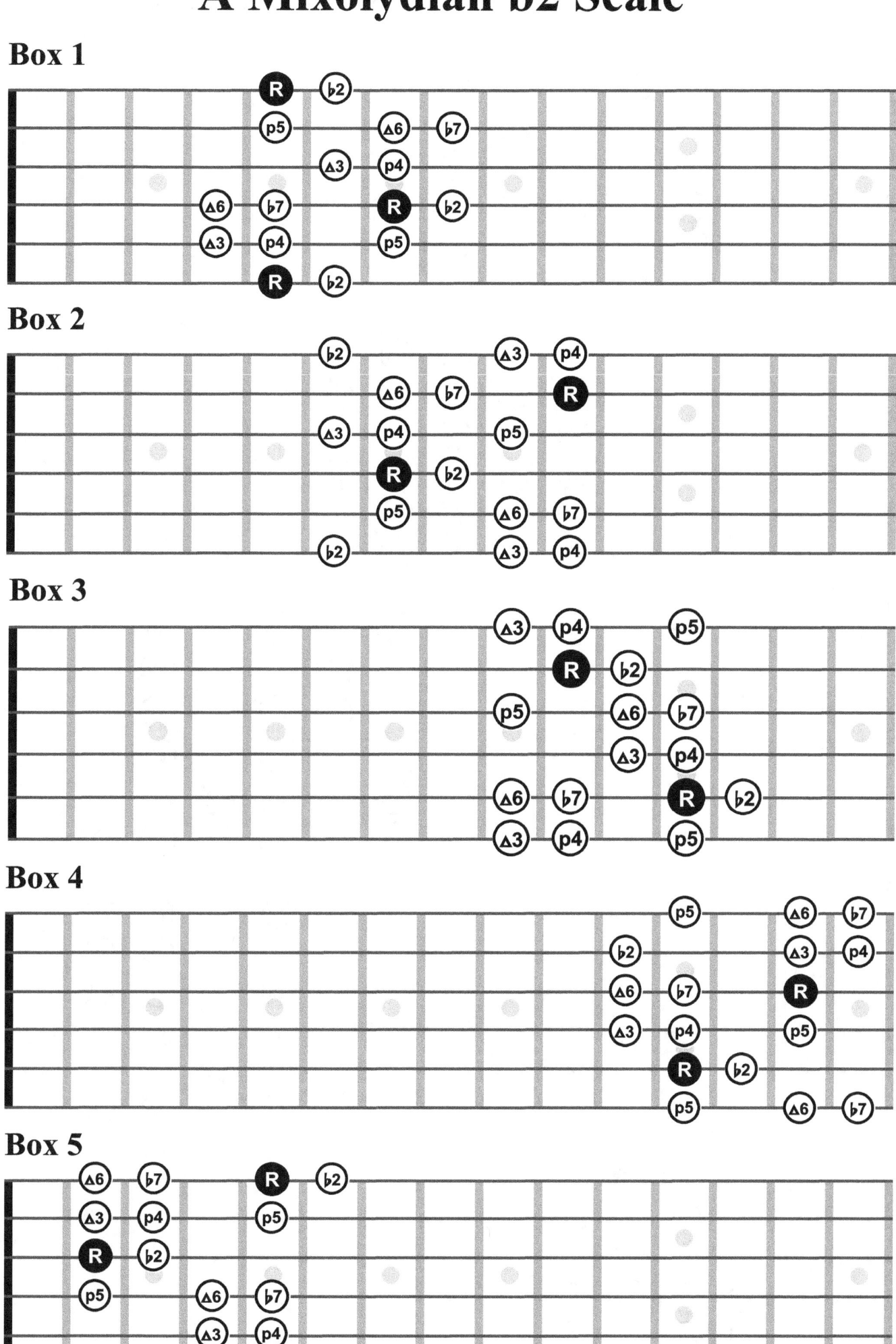

A Lydian Augmented #2 Scale

Box 1

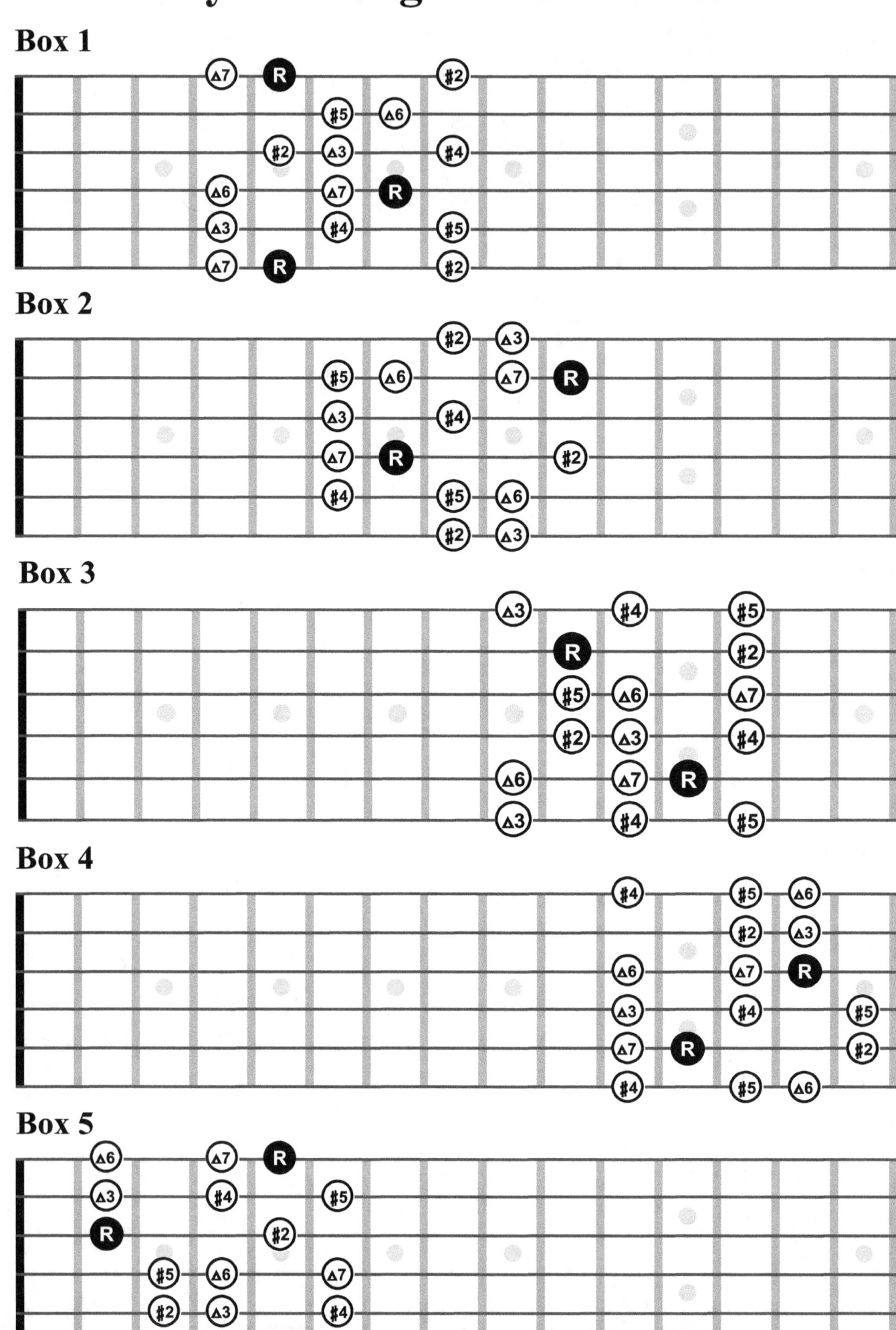

Box 2

Box 3

Box 4

Box 5

A Locrian bb7 Scale

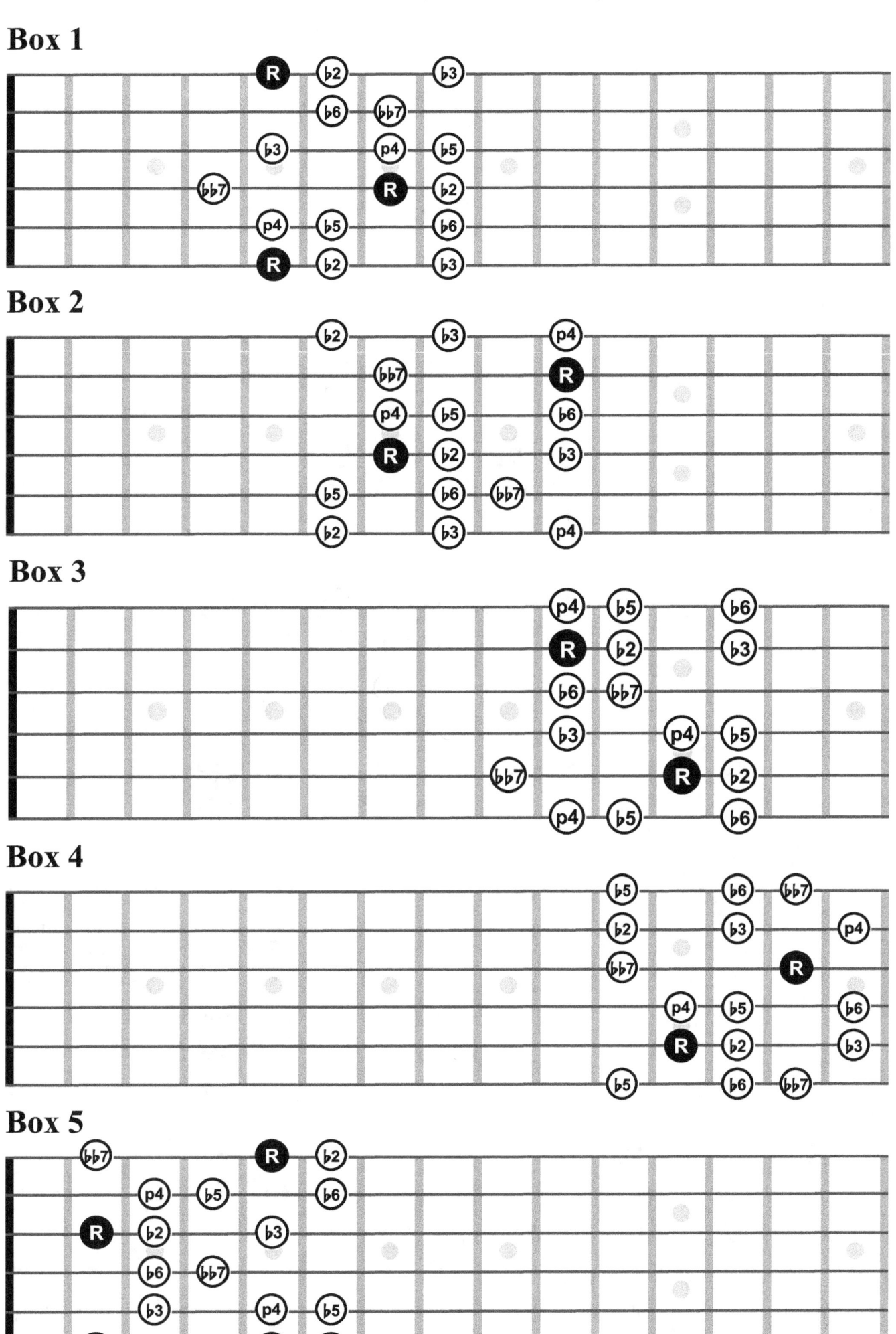

A Neapolitan Major Scale

Box 1

Box 2

Box 3

Box 4

Box 5

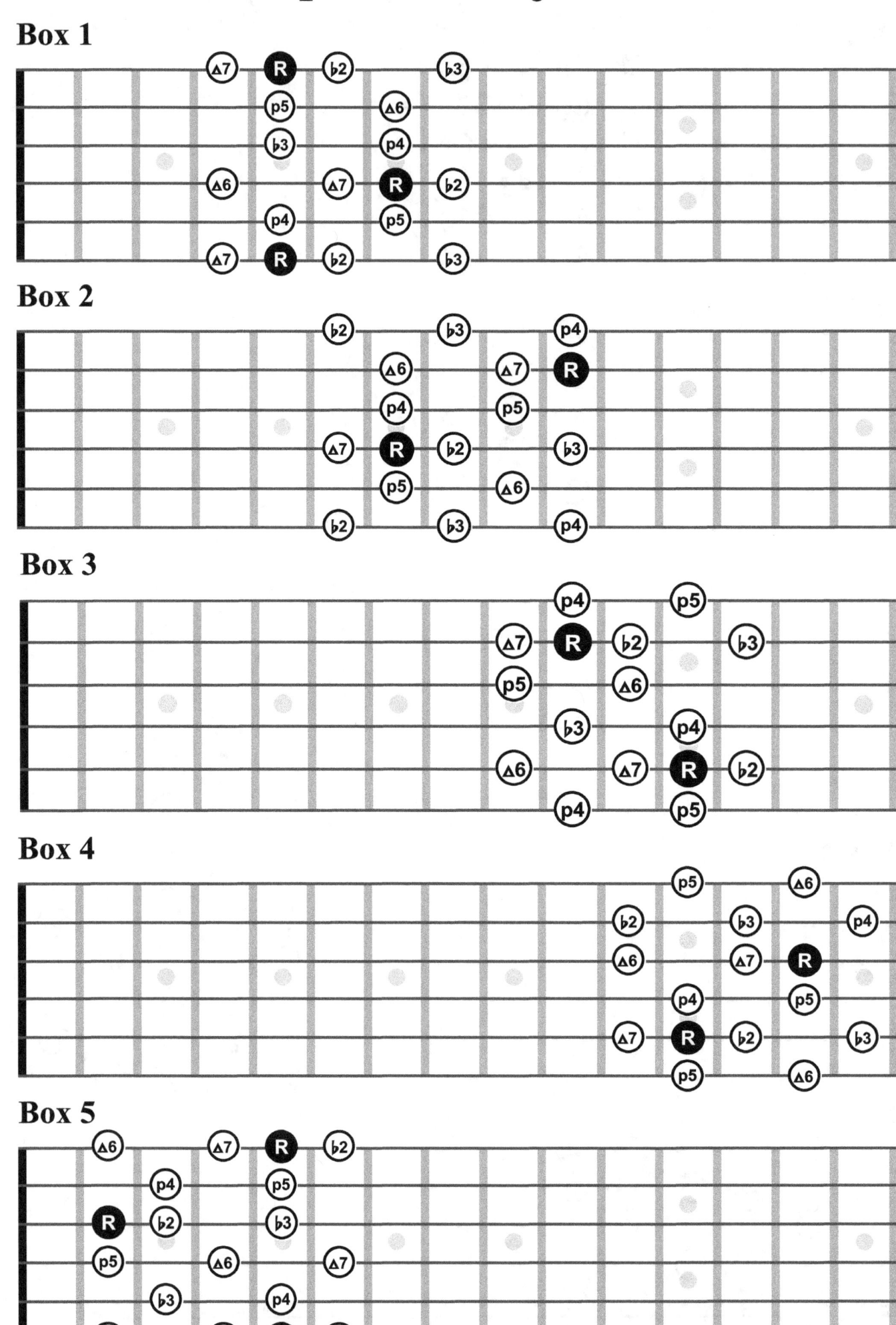

A Leading Whole Tone Scale

Box 1

Box 2

Box 3

Box 4

Box 5

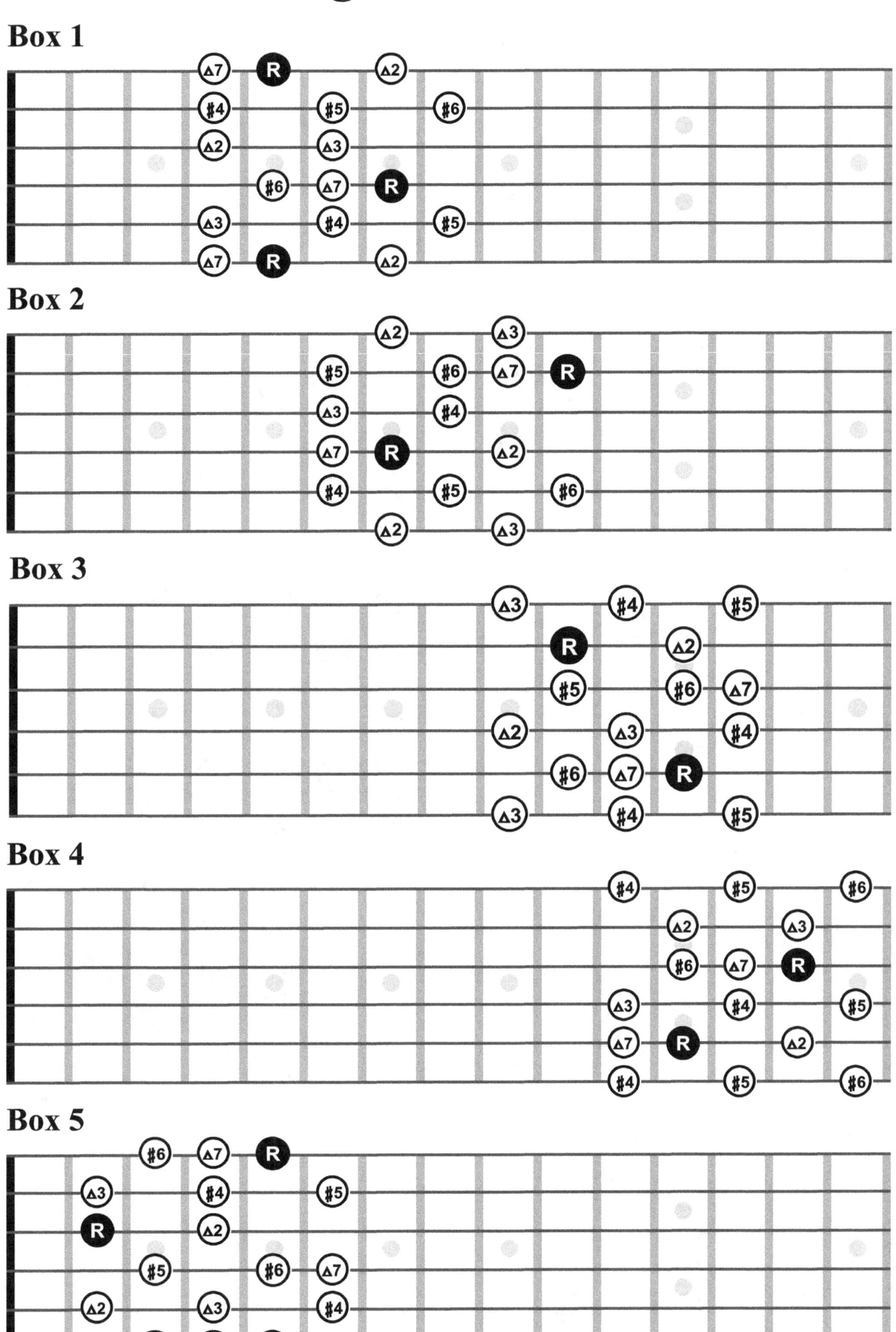

A Lydian Augmented Dominant Scale

Box 1

Box 2

Box 3

Box 4

Box 5

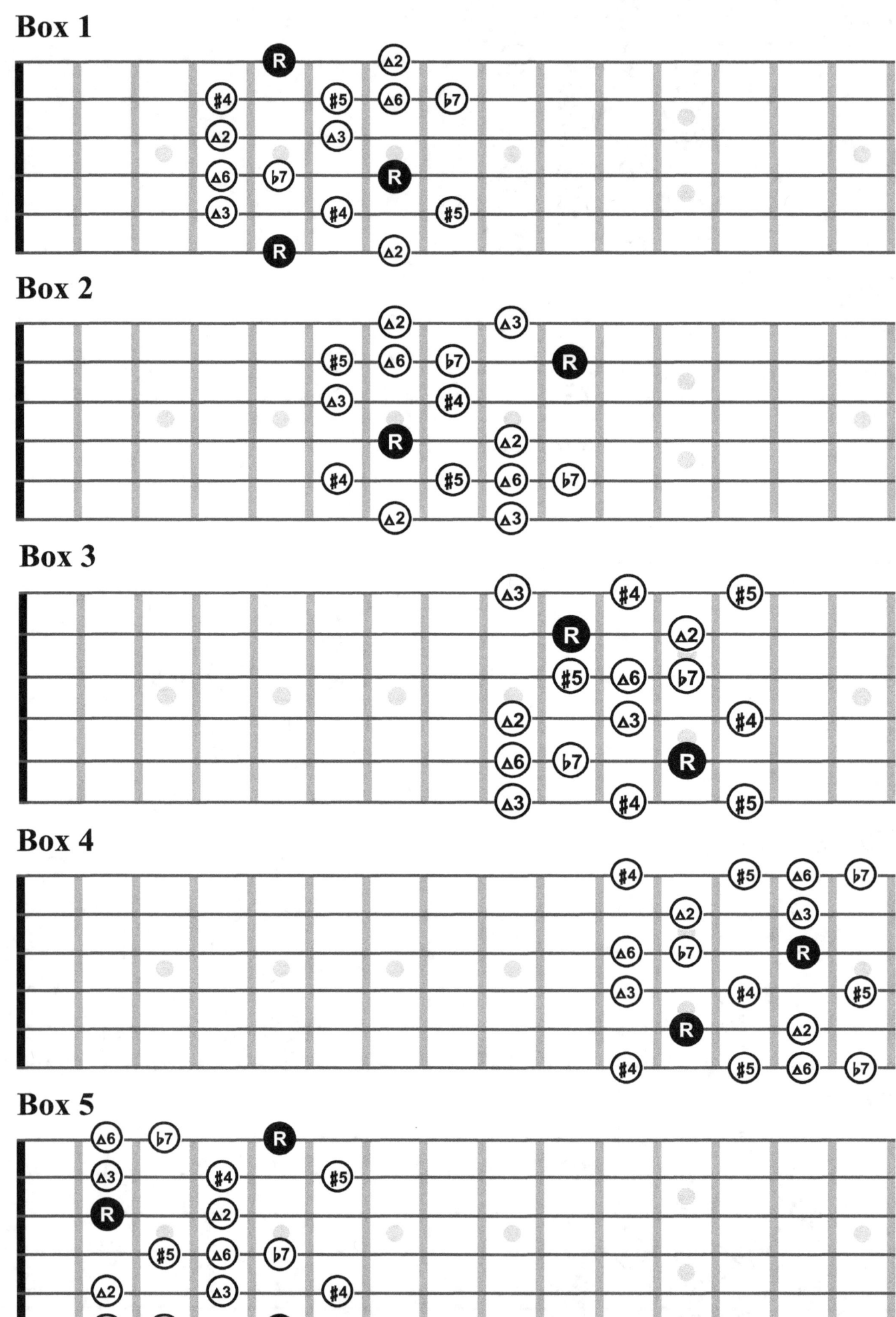

A Lydian Minor Scale

Box 1

Box 2

Box 3

Box 4

Box 5

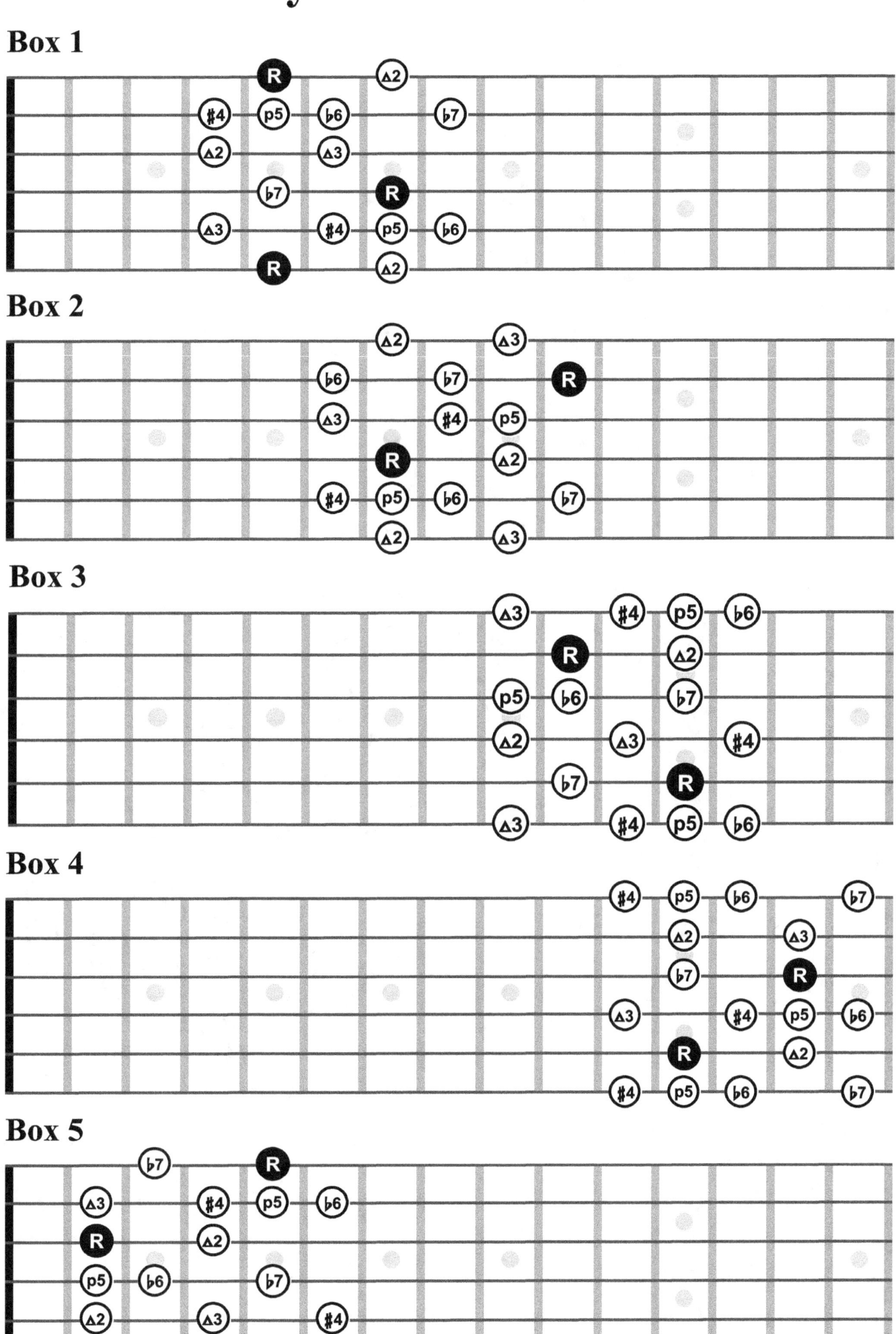

A Major Locrian Scale

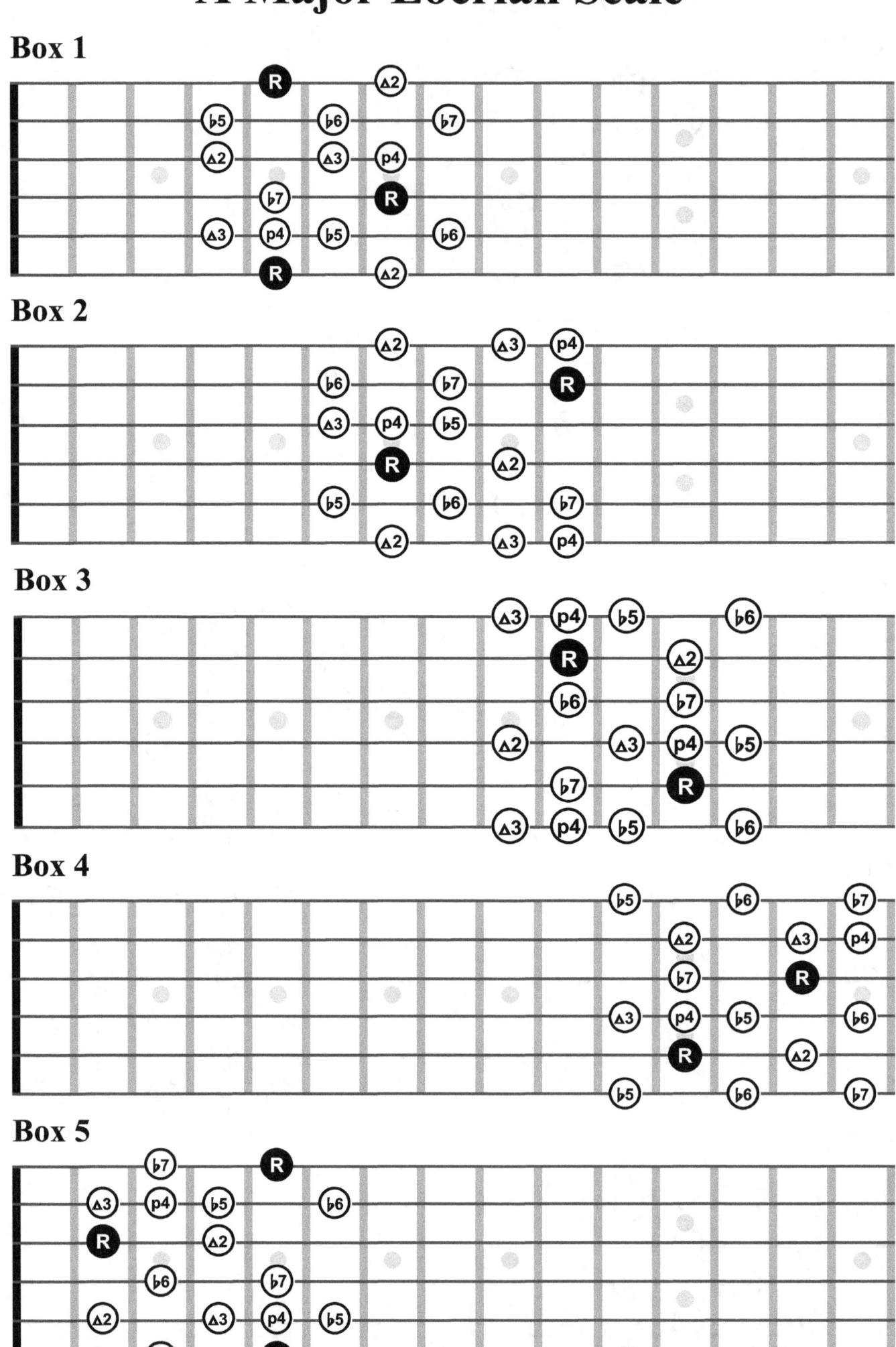

A Altered Natural 2 Scale

Box 1

Box 2

Box 3

Box 4

Box 5

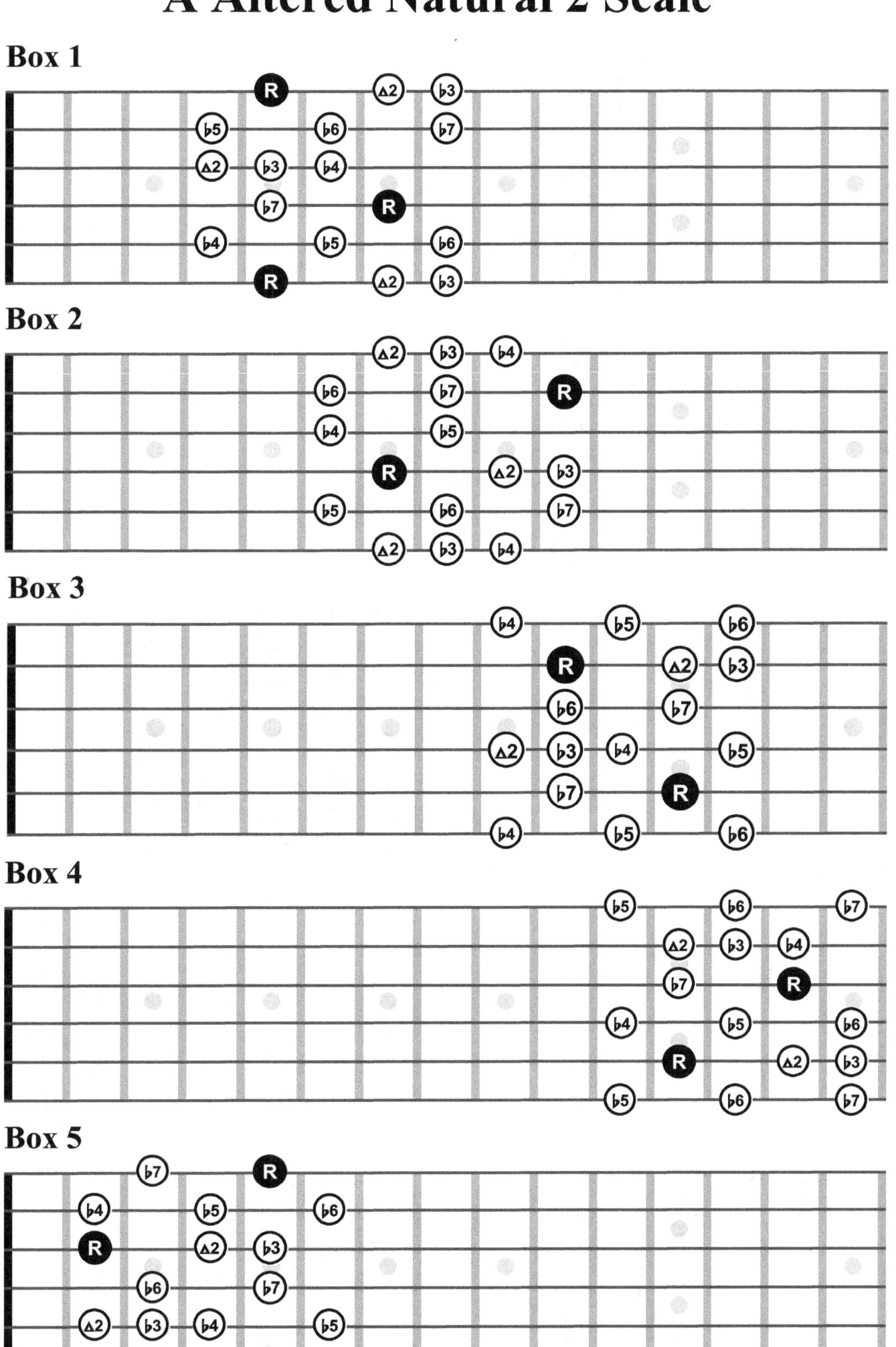

A Altered bb3 Scale

Box 1

Box 2

Box 3

Box 4

Box 5

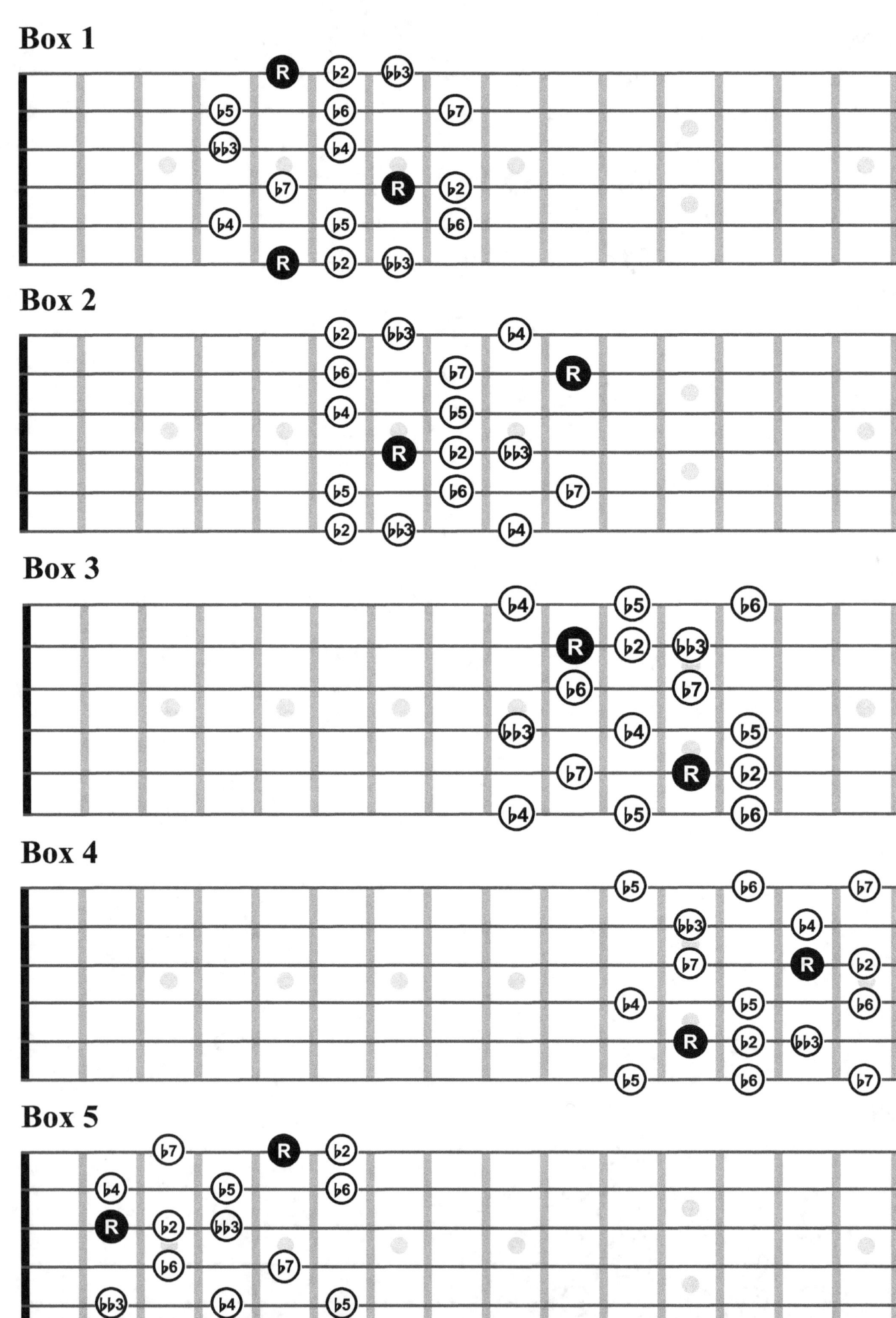

A Neapolitan Minor Scale

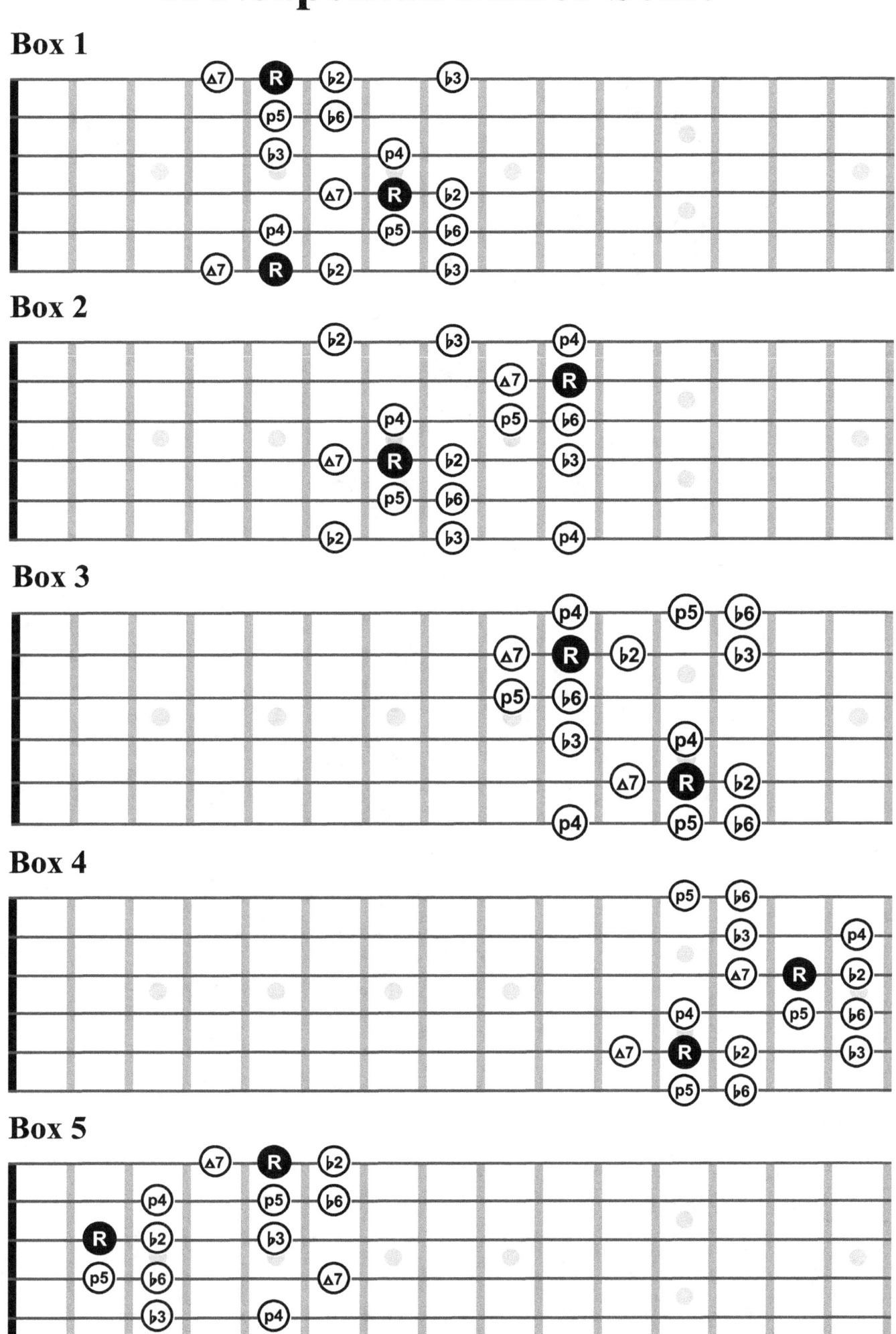

A Lydian #6 Scale

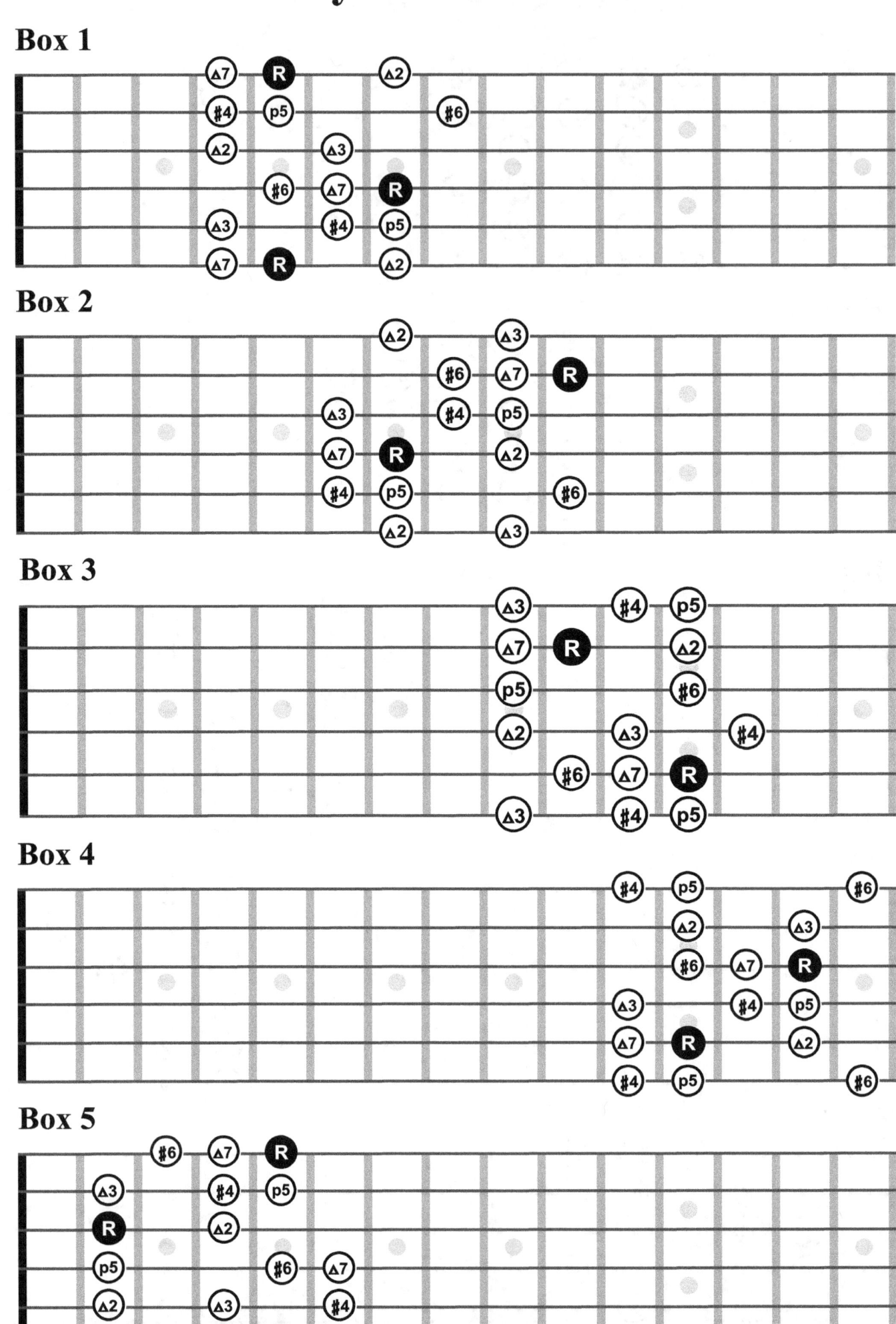

Box 1

Box 2

Box 3

Box 4

Box 5

A Dominant Augmented Scale

Box 1

Box 2

Box 3

Box 4

Box 5

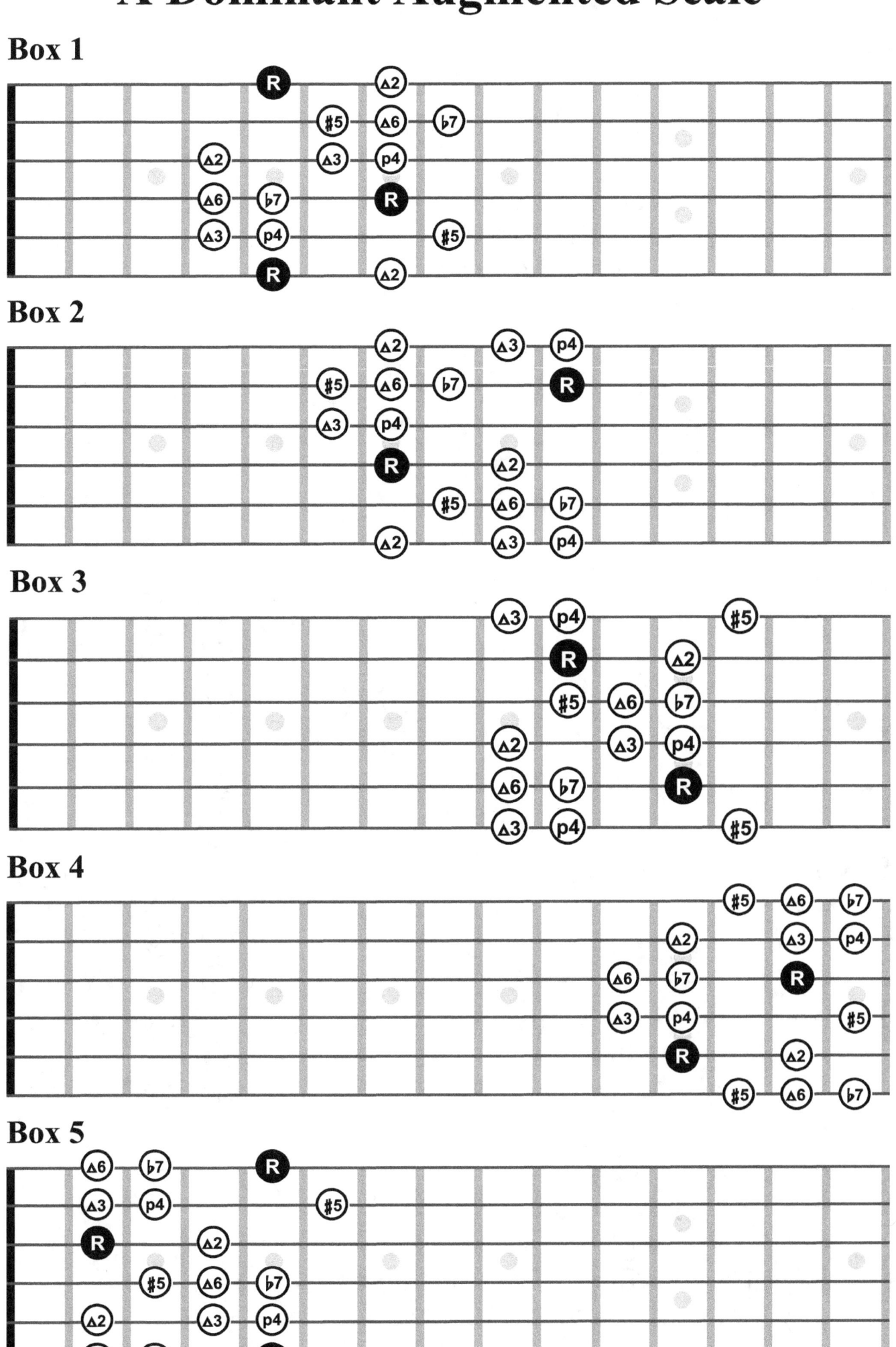

A Hungarian Gypsy Scale

Box 1

Box 2

Box 3

Box 4

Box 5

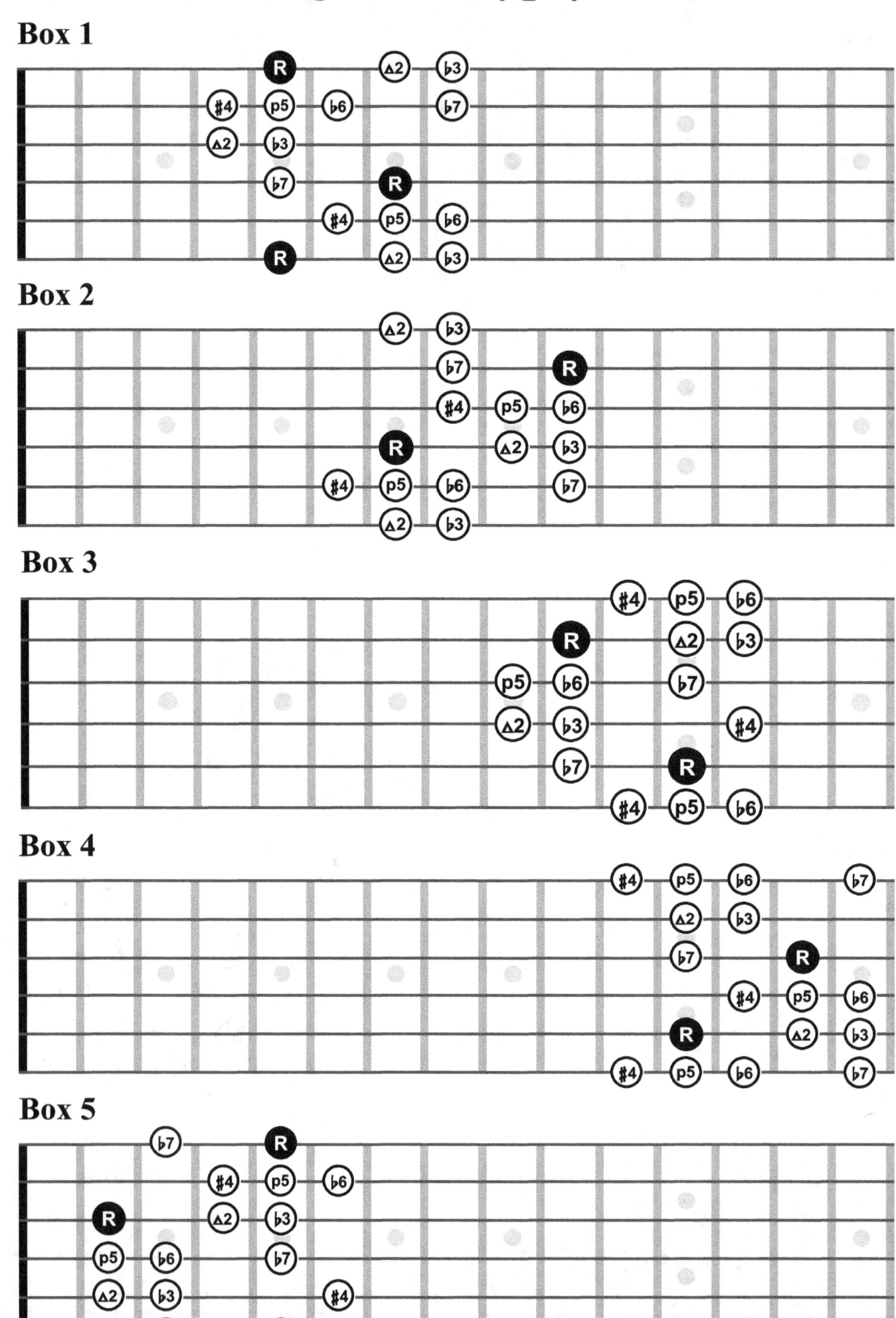

A Locrian Natural 3 Scale

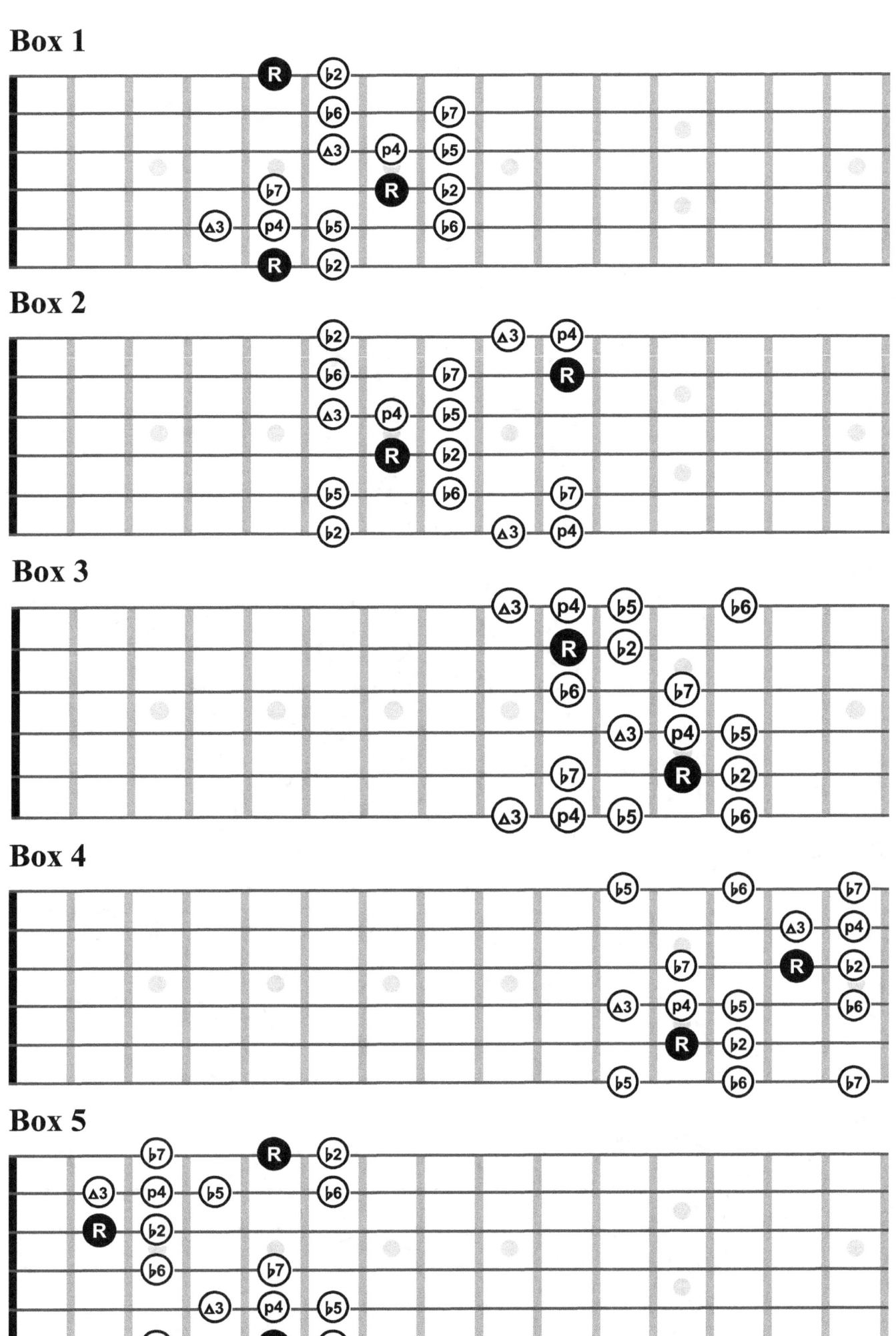

A Ionian #2 Scale

Box 1

Box 2

Box 3

Box 4

Box 5

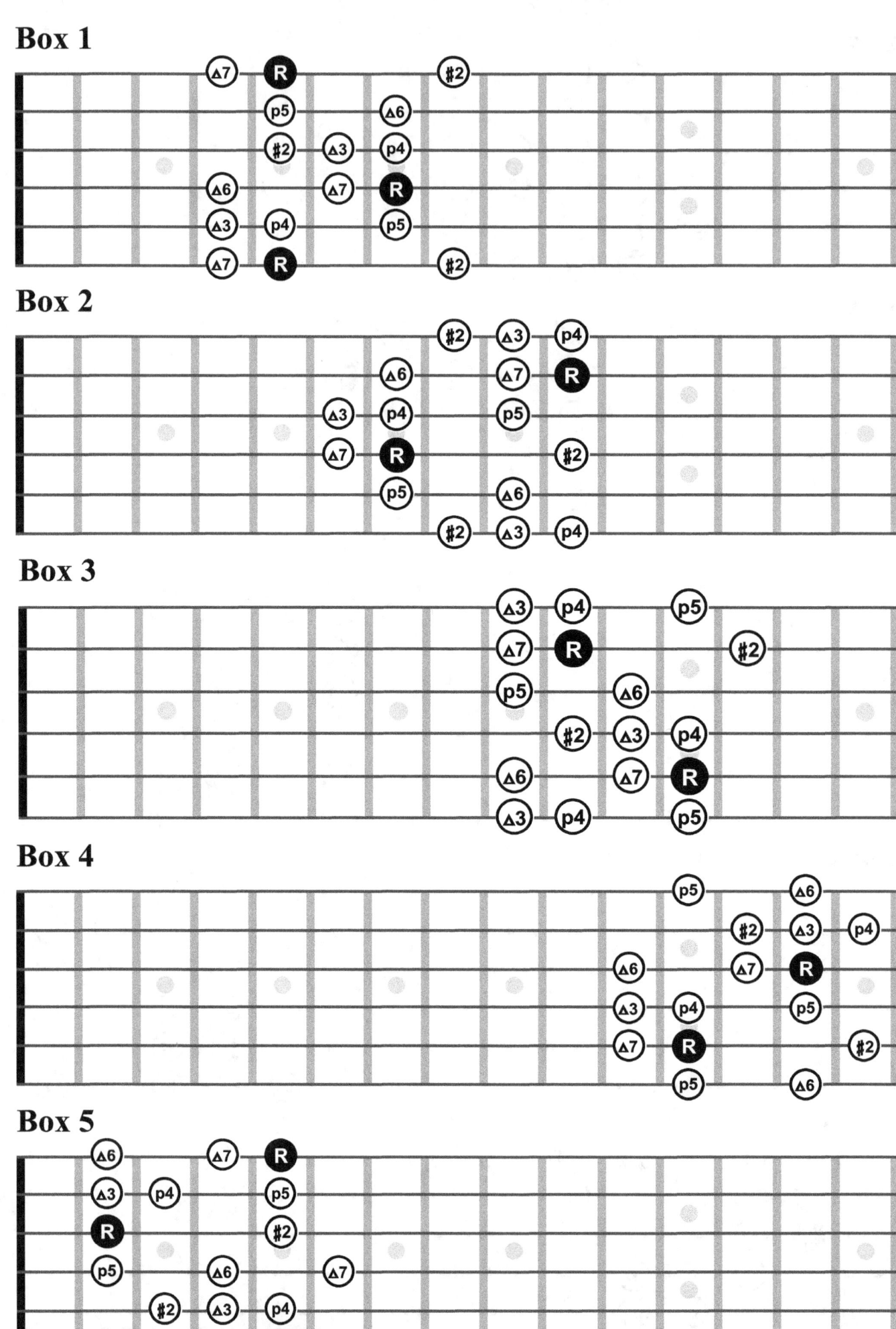

A Altered bb3 bb7 Scale

Box 1

Box 2

Box 3

Box 4

Box 5

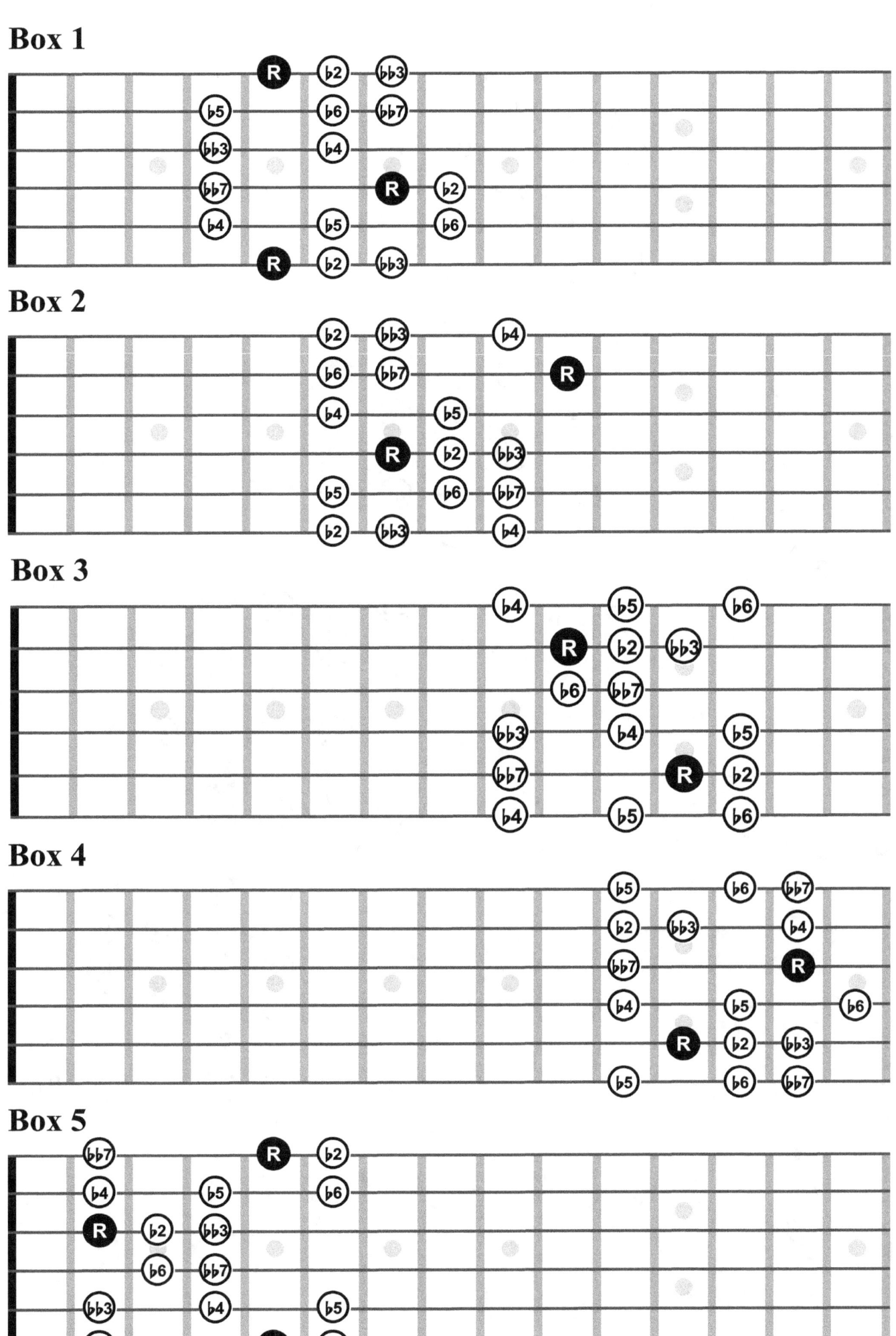

A Hungarian Scale

Box 1

Box 2

Box 3

Box 4

Box 5

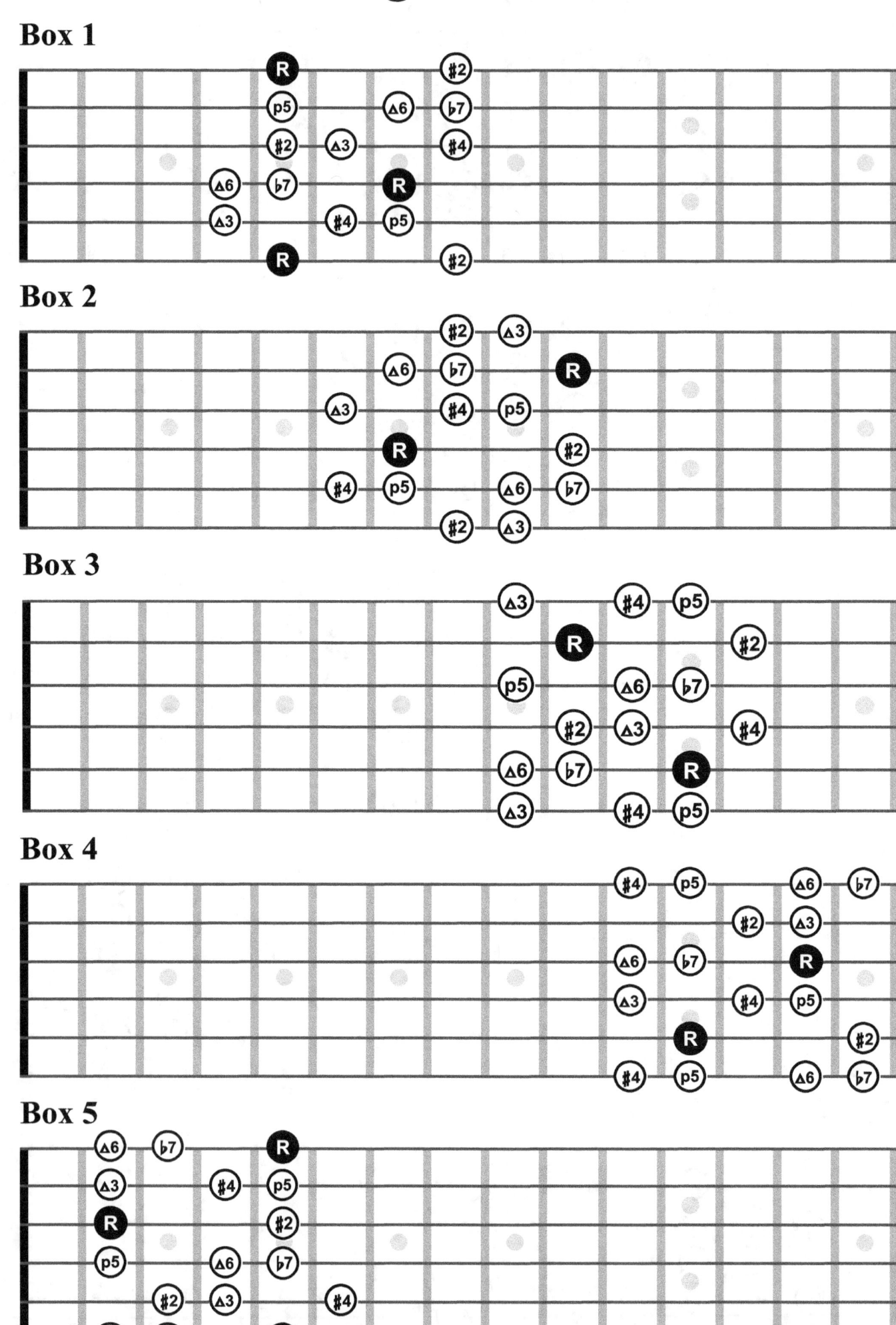

A Altered bb6 bb7 Scale

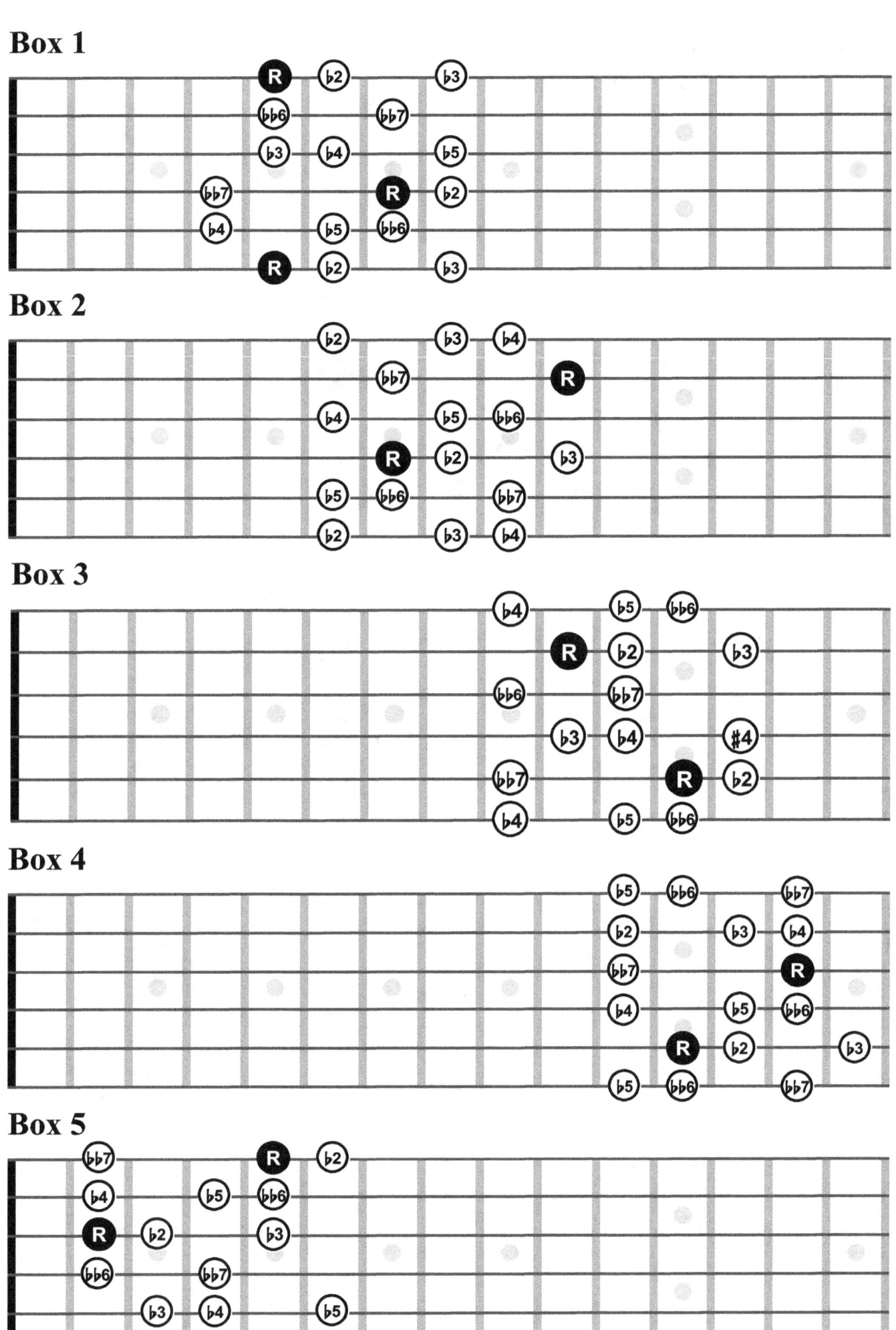

A Locrian Natural 2 Natural 7 Scale

Box 1

Box 2

Box 3

Box 4

Box 5

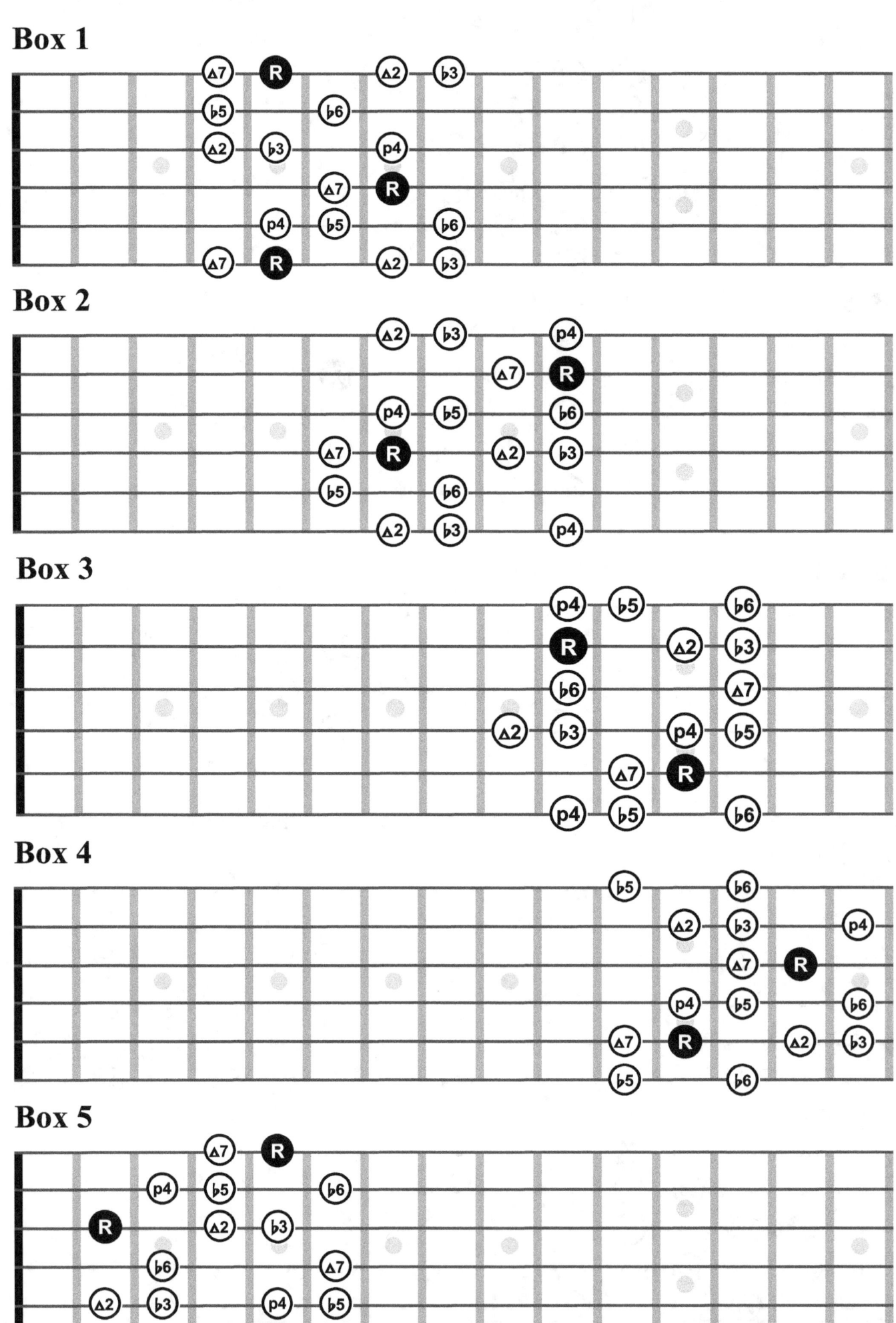

A Altered Natural 6 Scale

Box 1

Box 2

Box 3

Box 4

Box 5

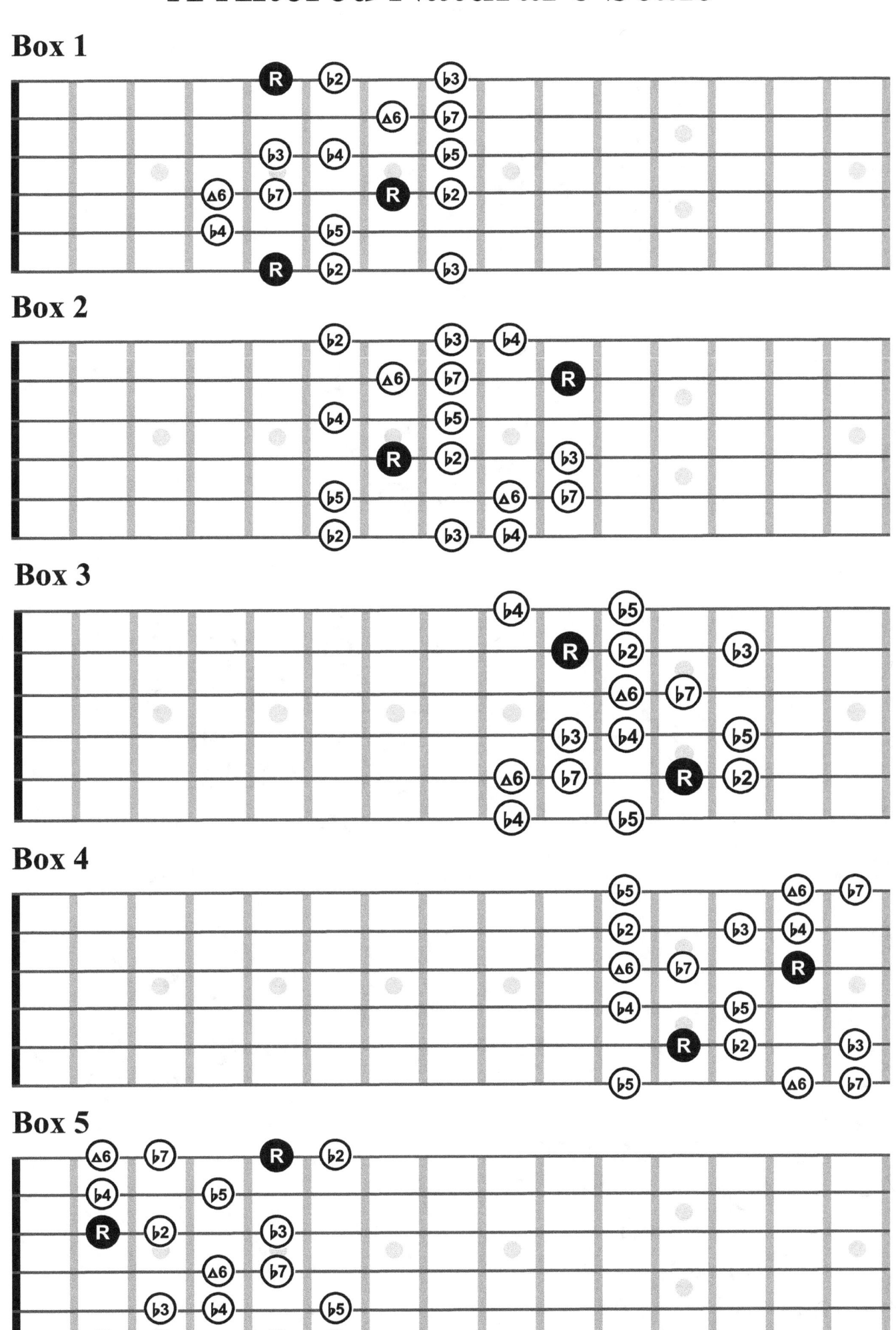

A Melodic Augmented Scale

Box 1

Box 2

Box 3

Box 4

Box 5

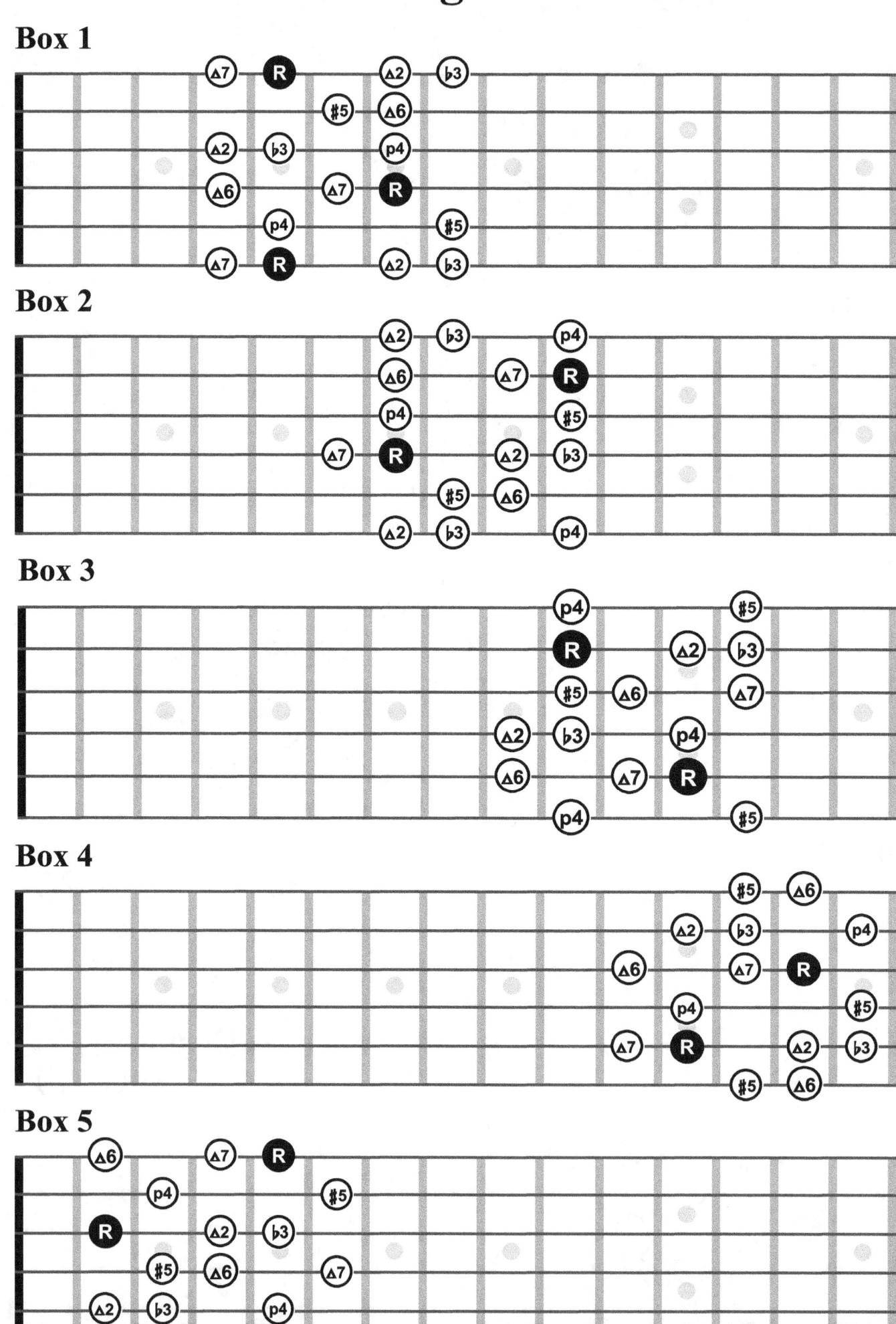

A Dorian b2 #4 Scale

Box 1

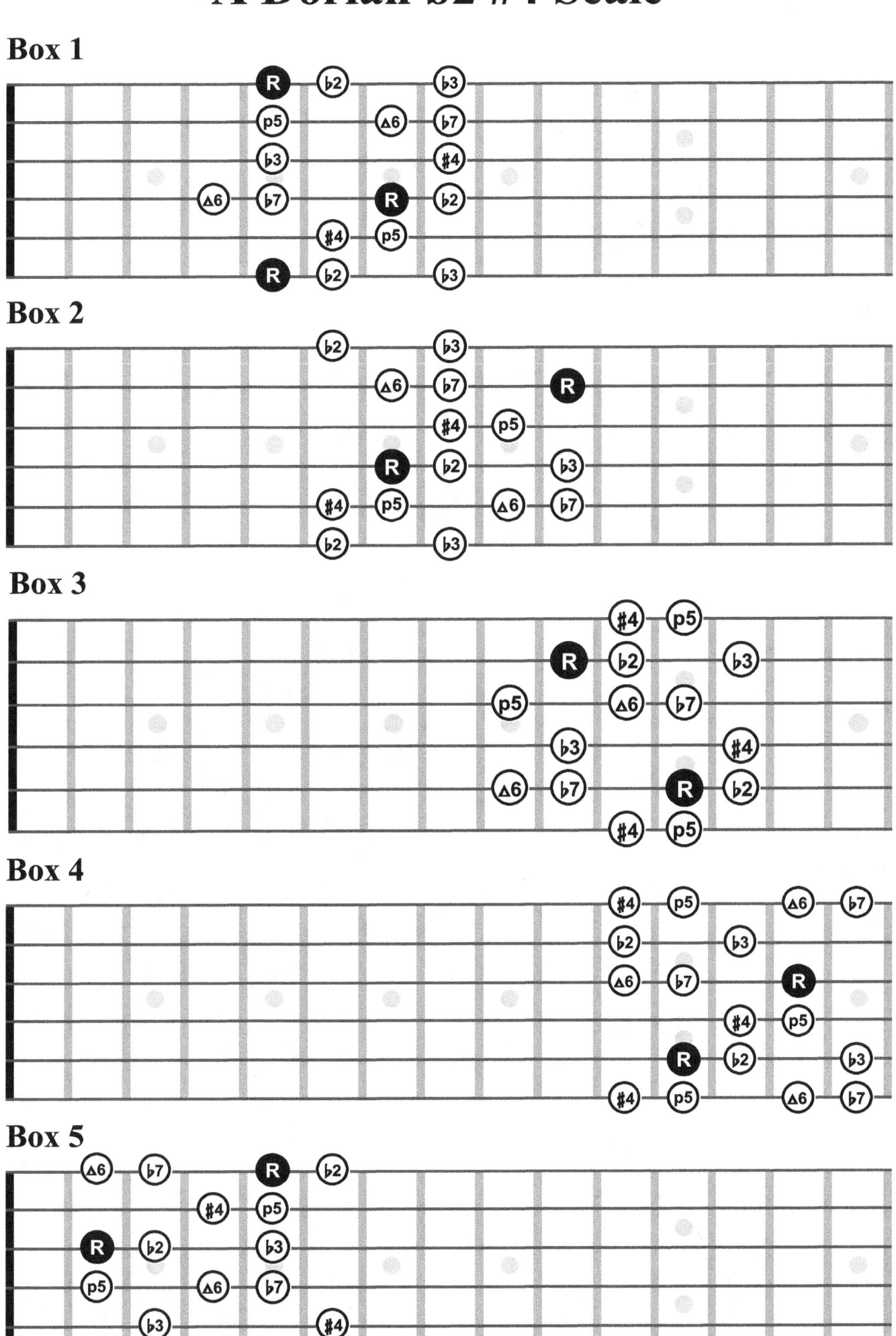

Box 2

Box 3

Box 4

Box 5

A Lydian Augmented #3 Scale

Box 1

Box 2

Box 3

Box 4

Box 5

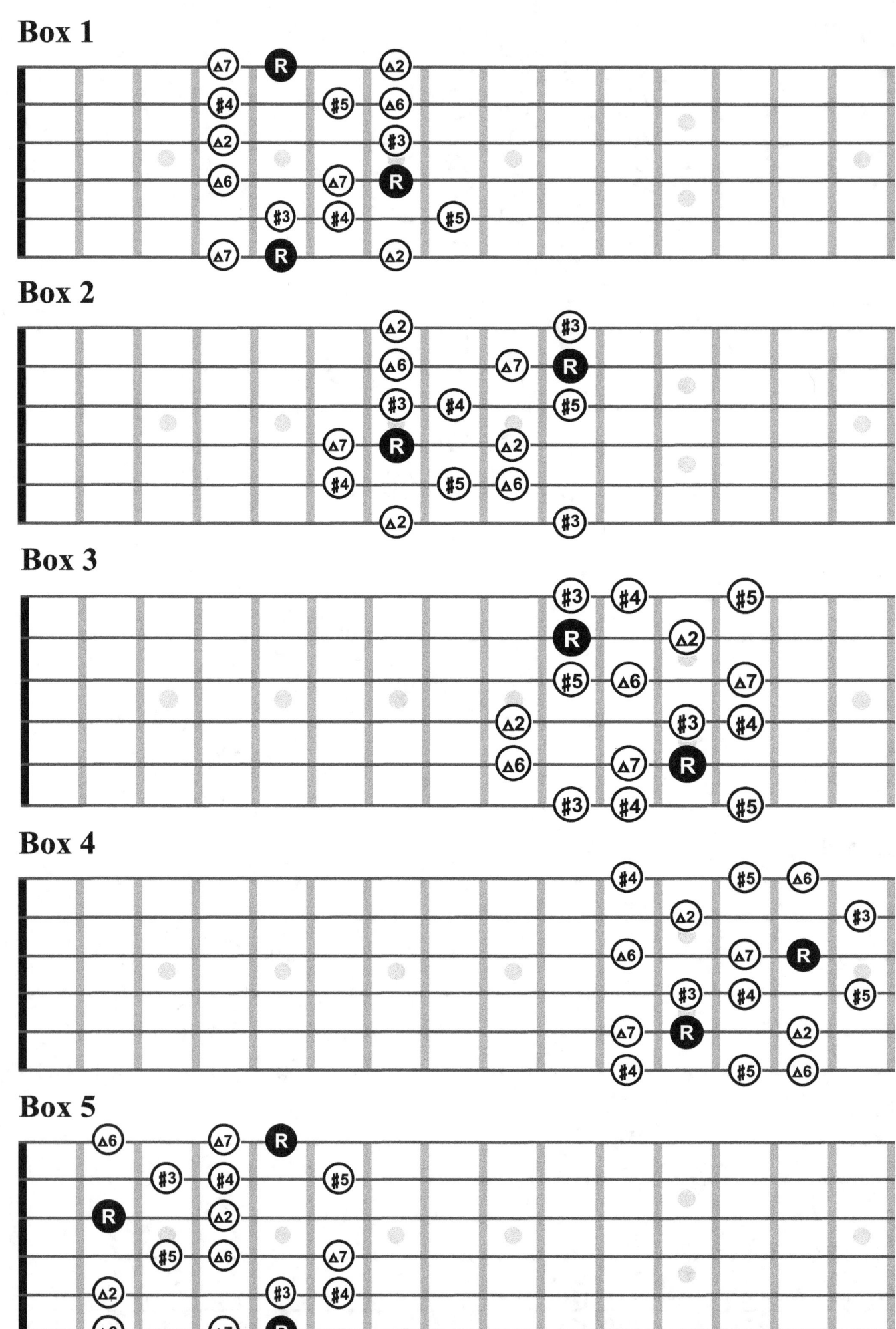

A Hungarian Minor Scale

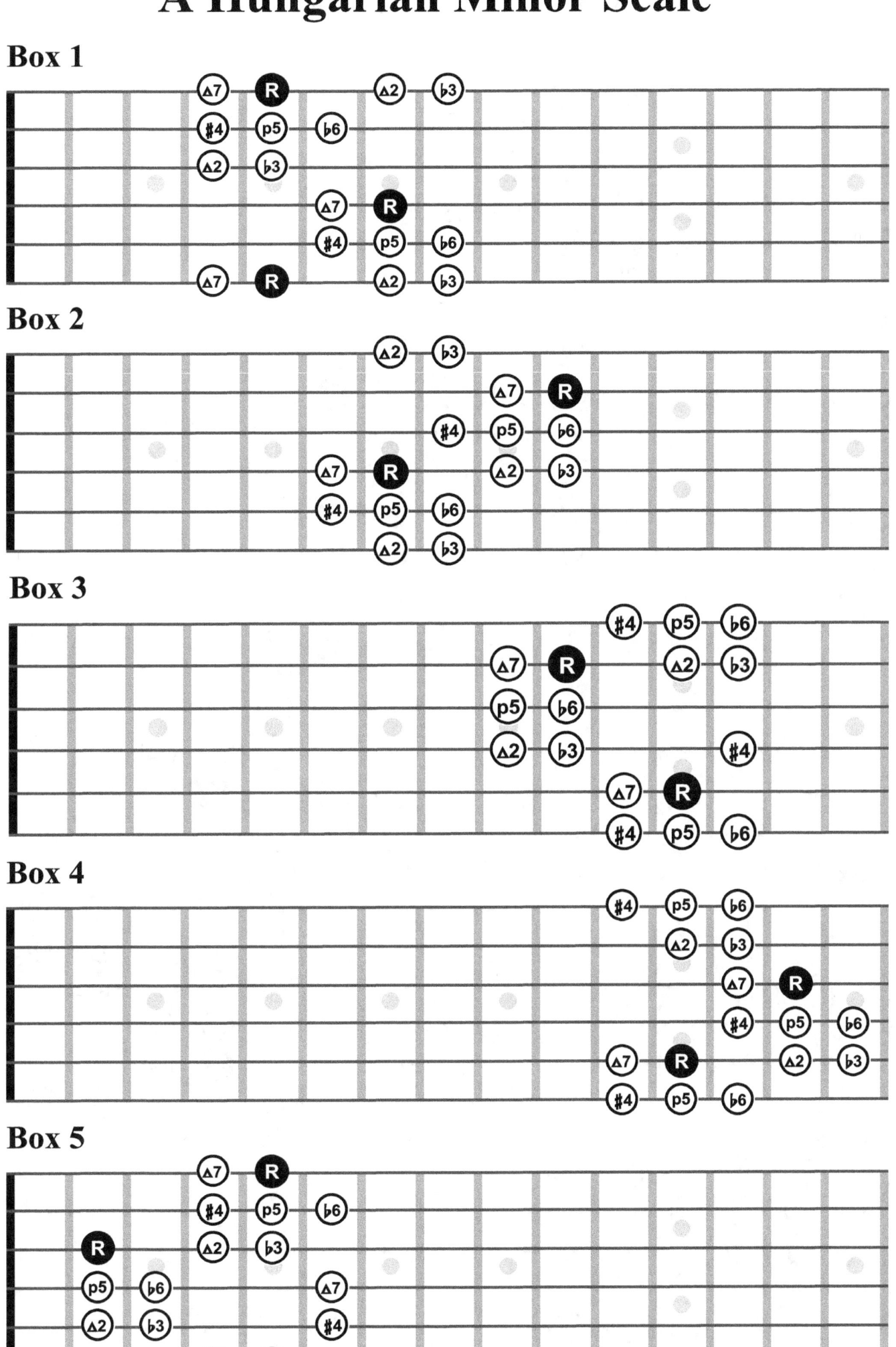

A Oriental Scale

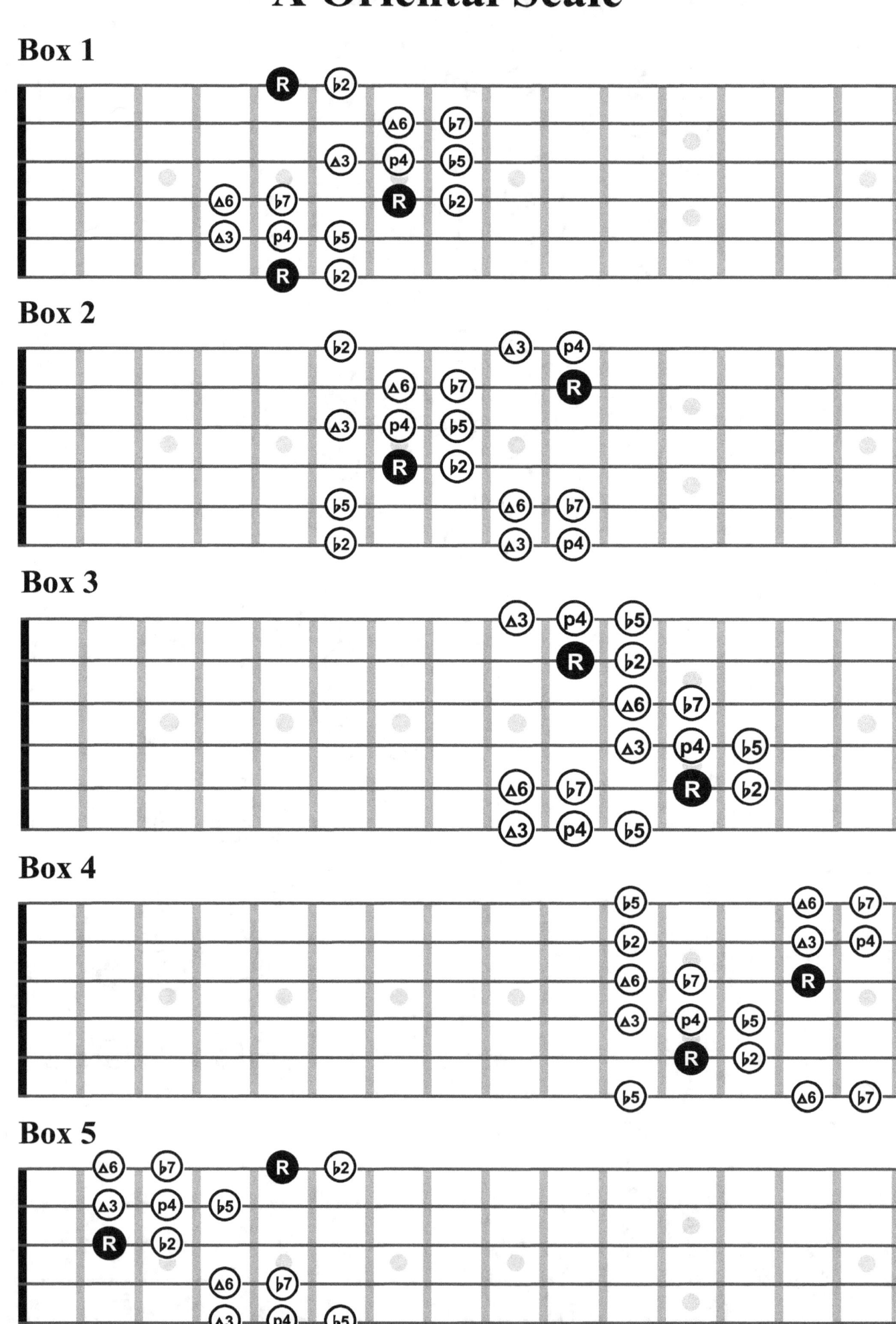

A Ionian Augmented #2 Scale

Box 1

Box 2

Box 3

Box 4

Box 5

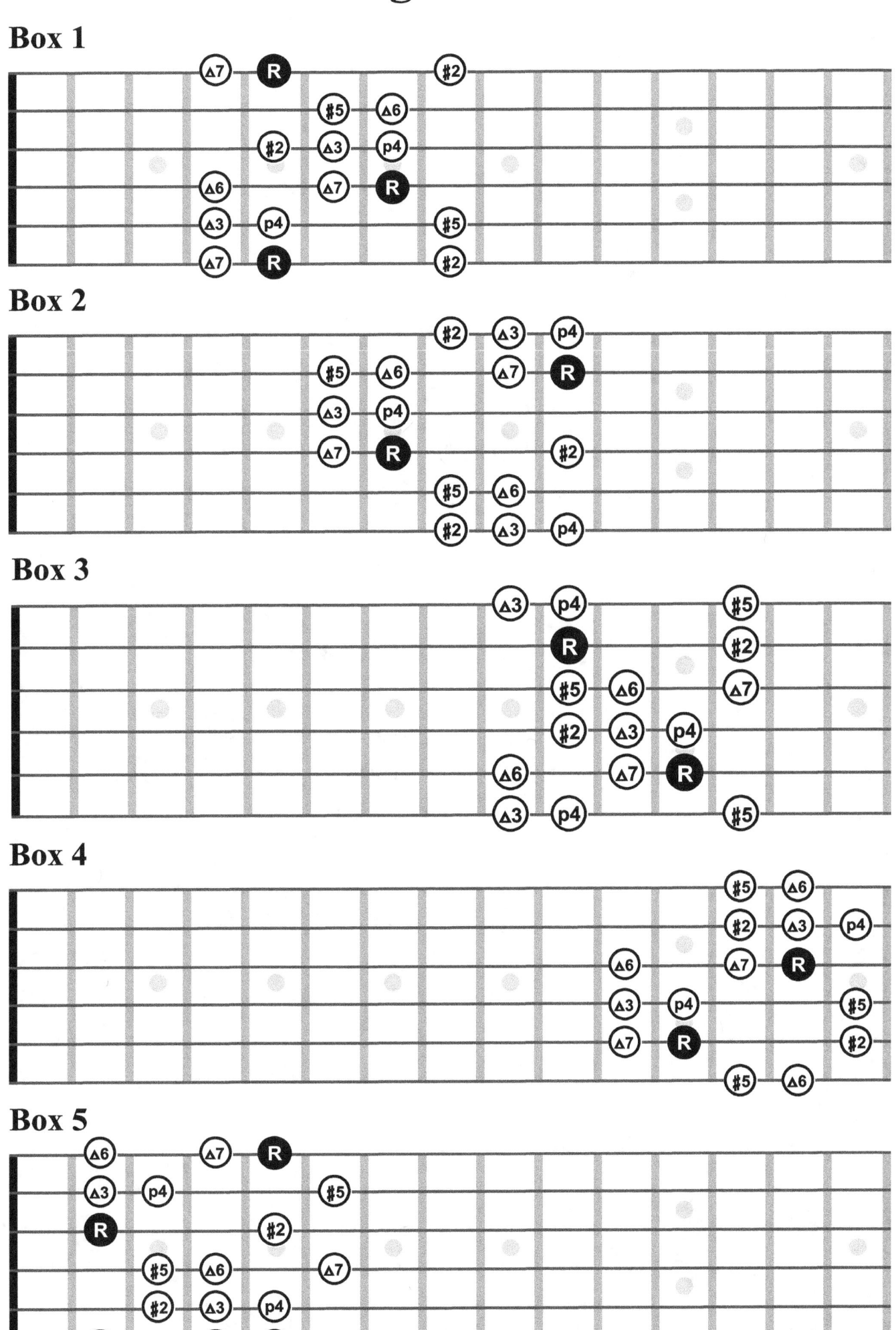

A Locrian bb3 bb7 Scale

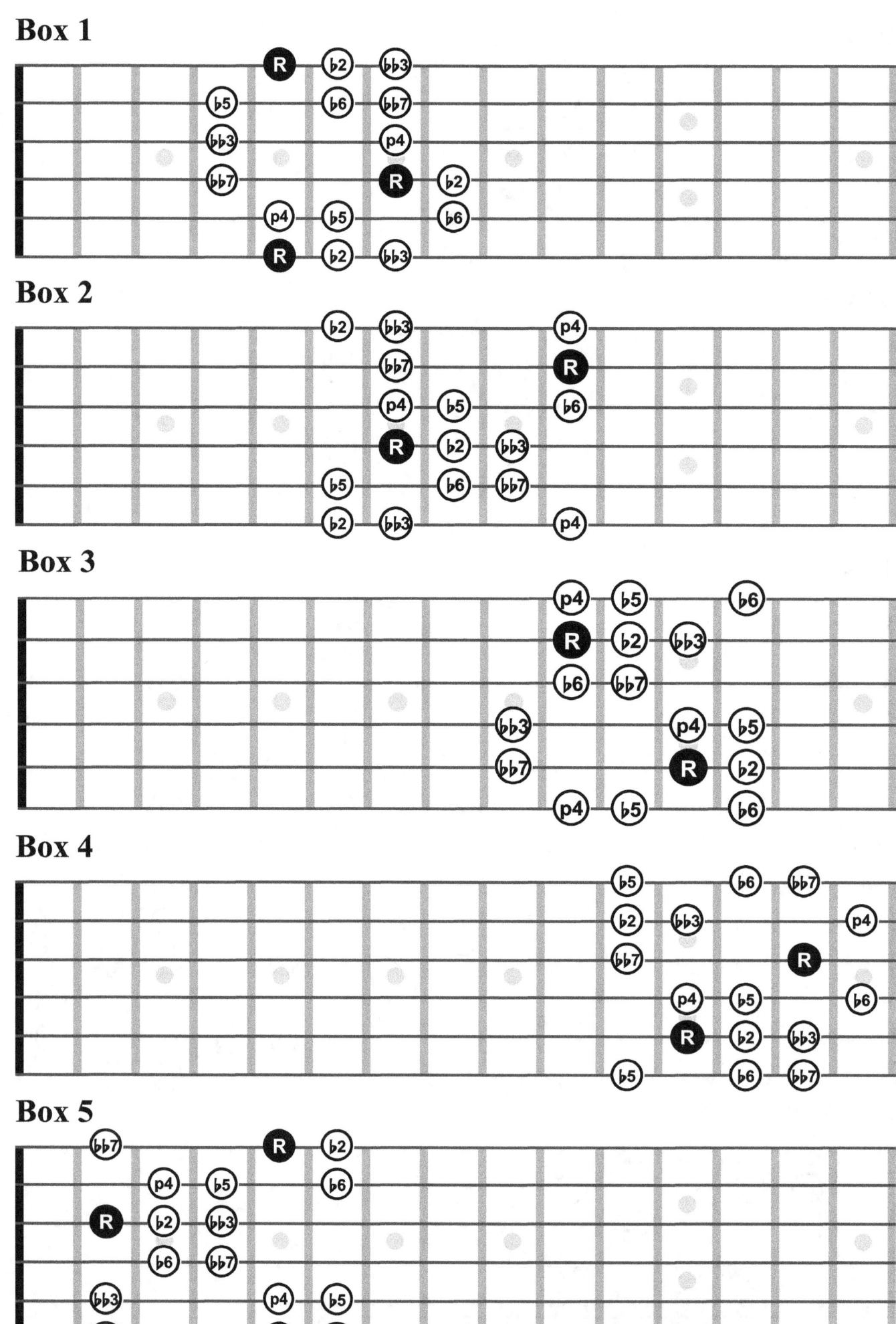

A Byzantine Scale

Box 1

Box 2

Box 3

Box 4

Box 5

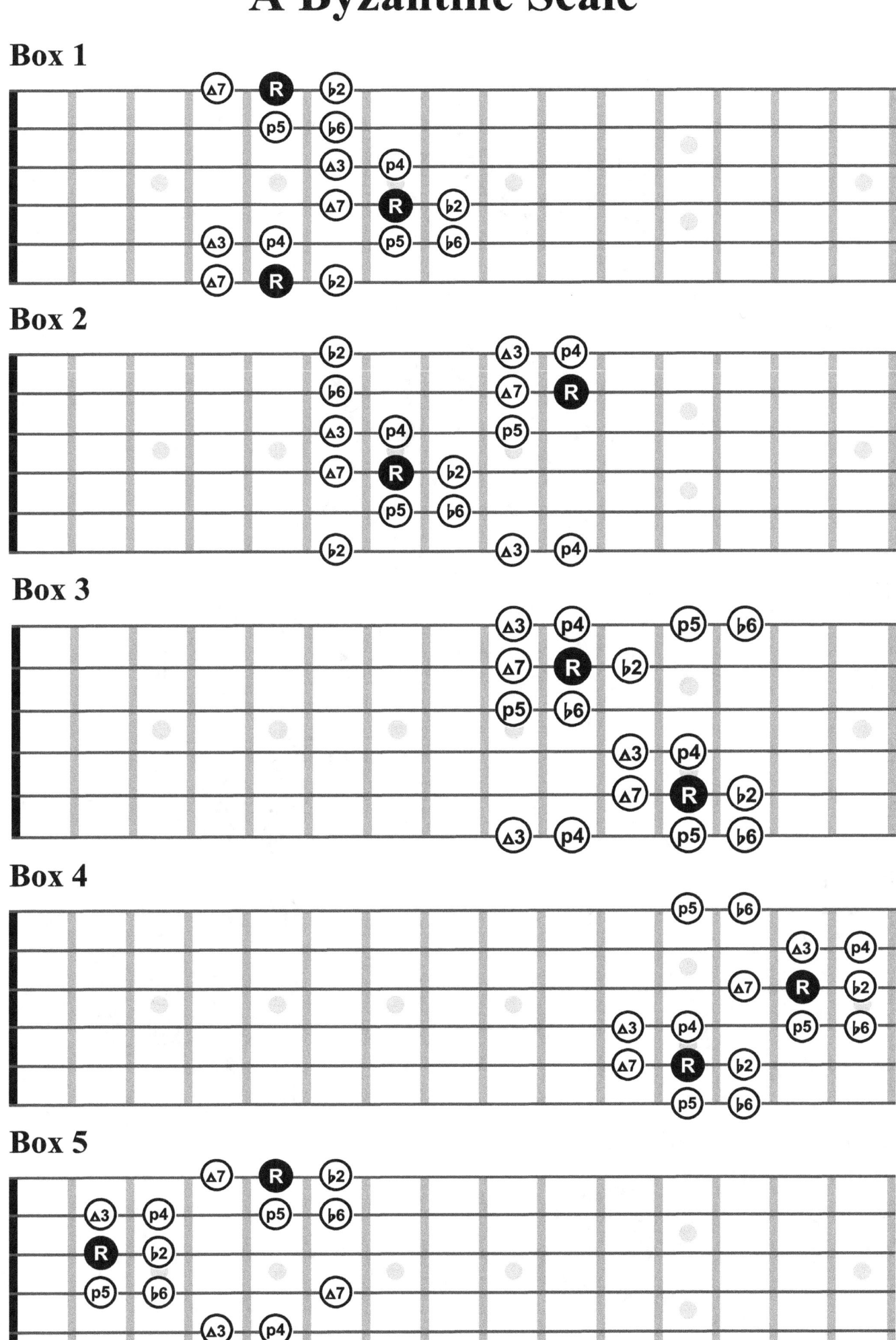

A Lydian #6 #2 Scale

Box 1

Box 2

Box 3

Box 4

Box 5

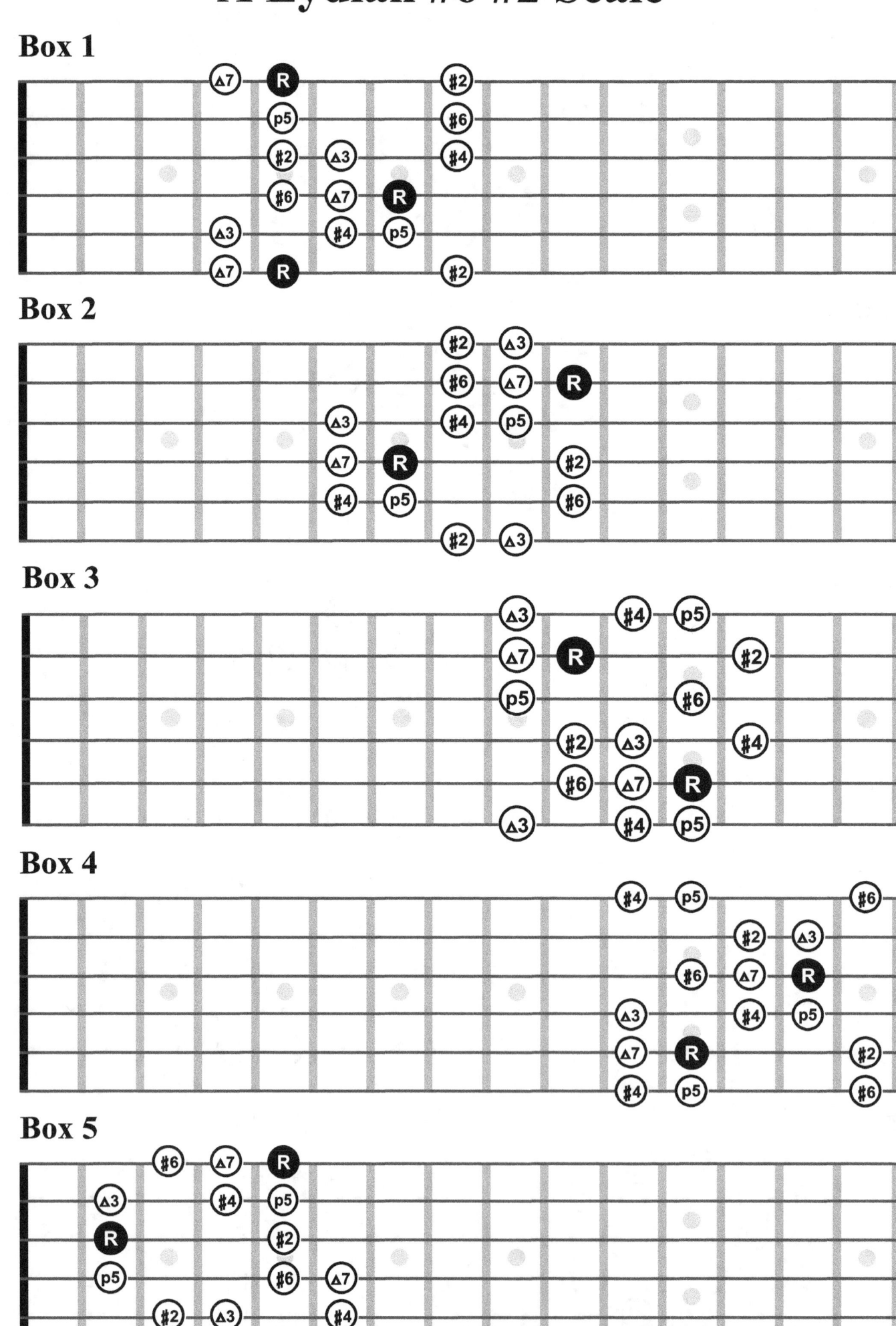

A Altered Natural 5 bb7 Scale

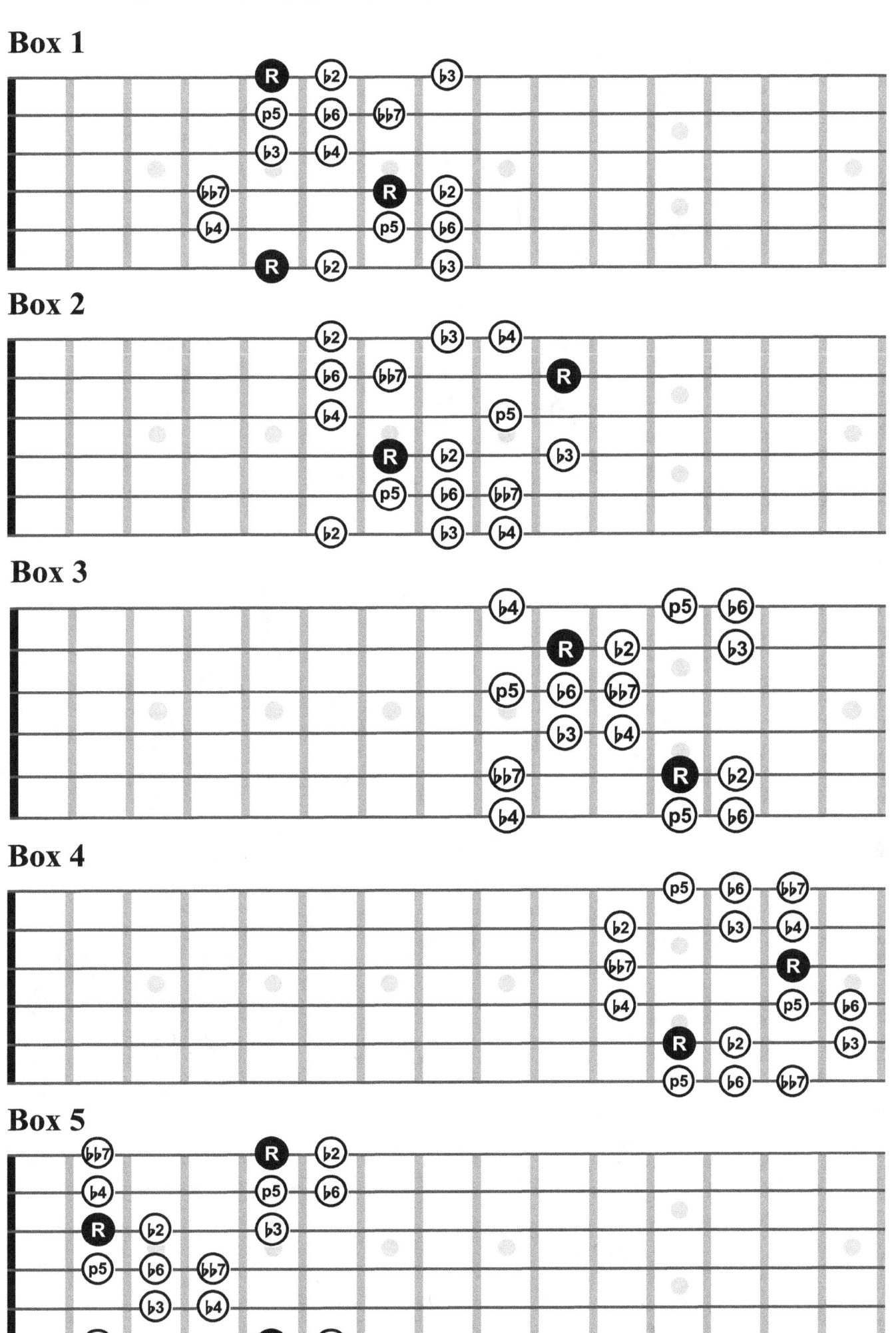

A Enigmatic Scale

Box 1

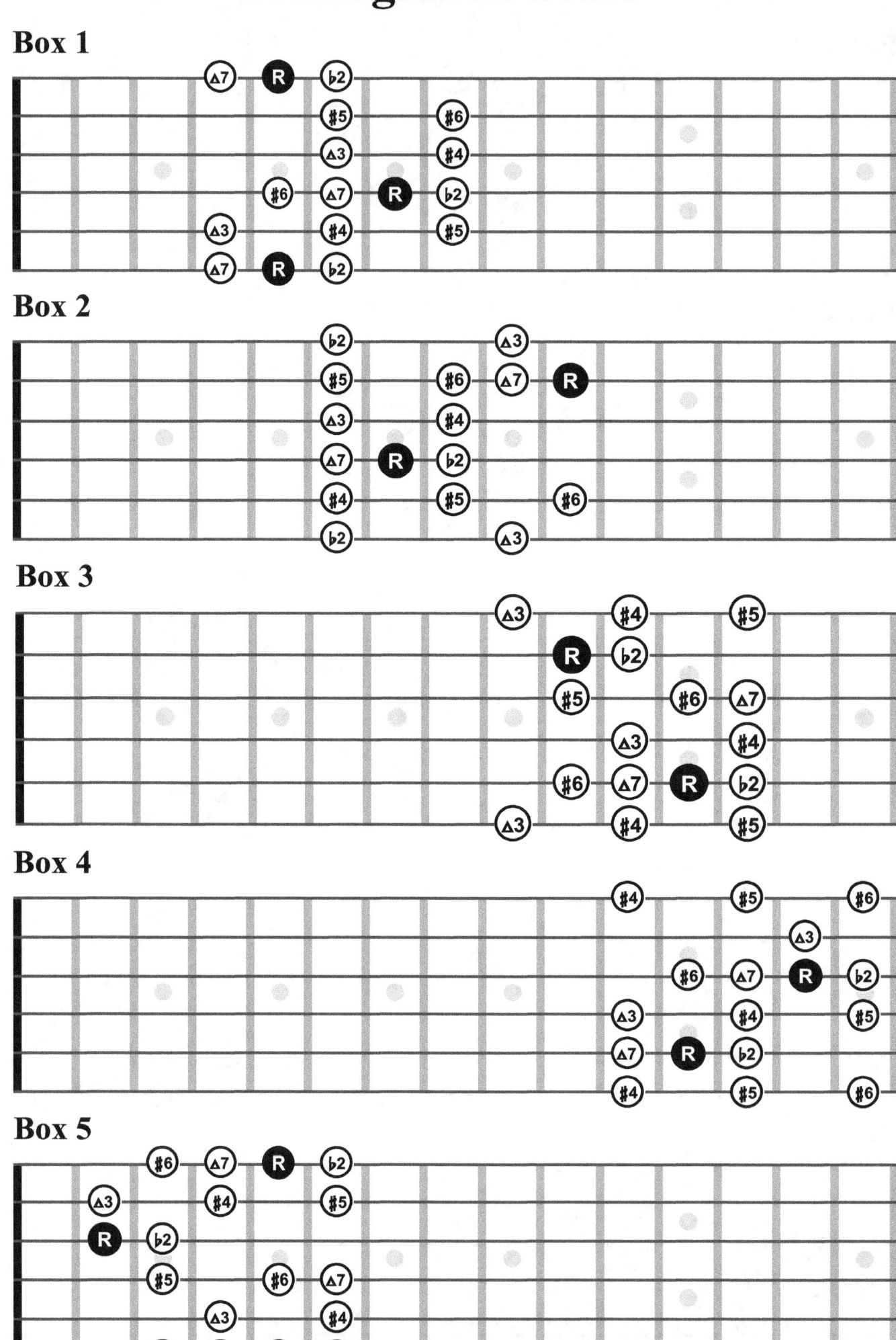

Box 2

Box 3

Box 4

Box 5

A Enigmatic Minor Scale

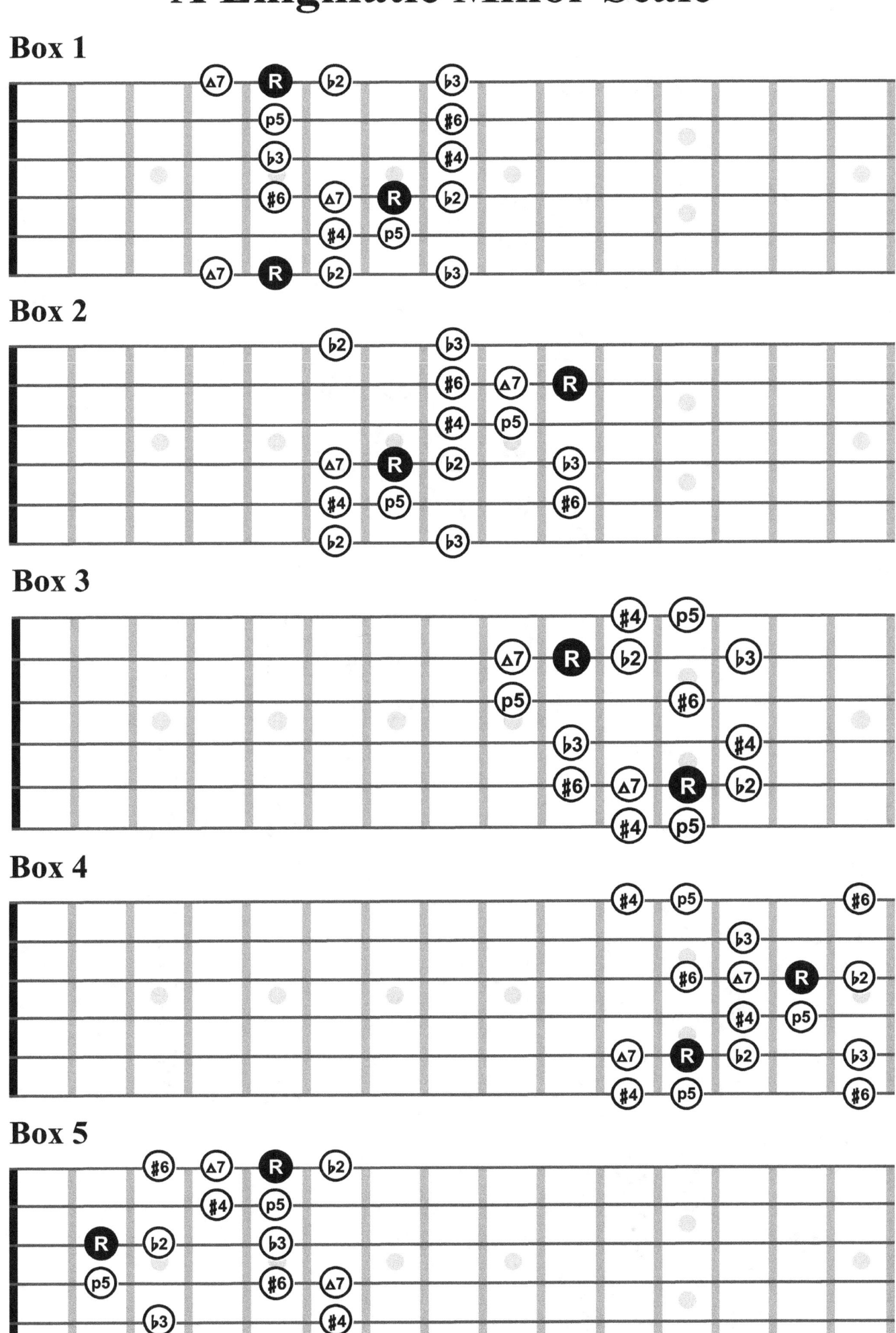

A Composite II Scale

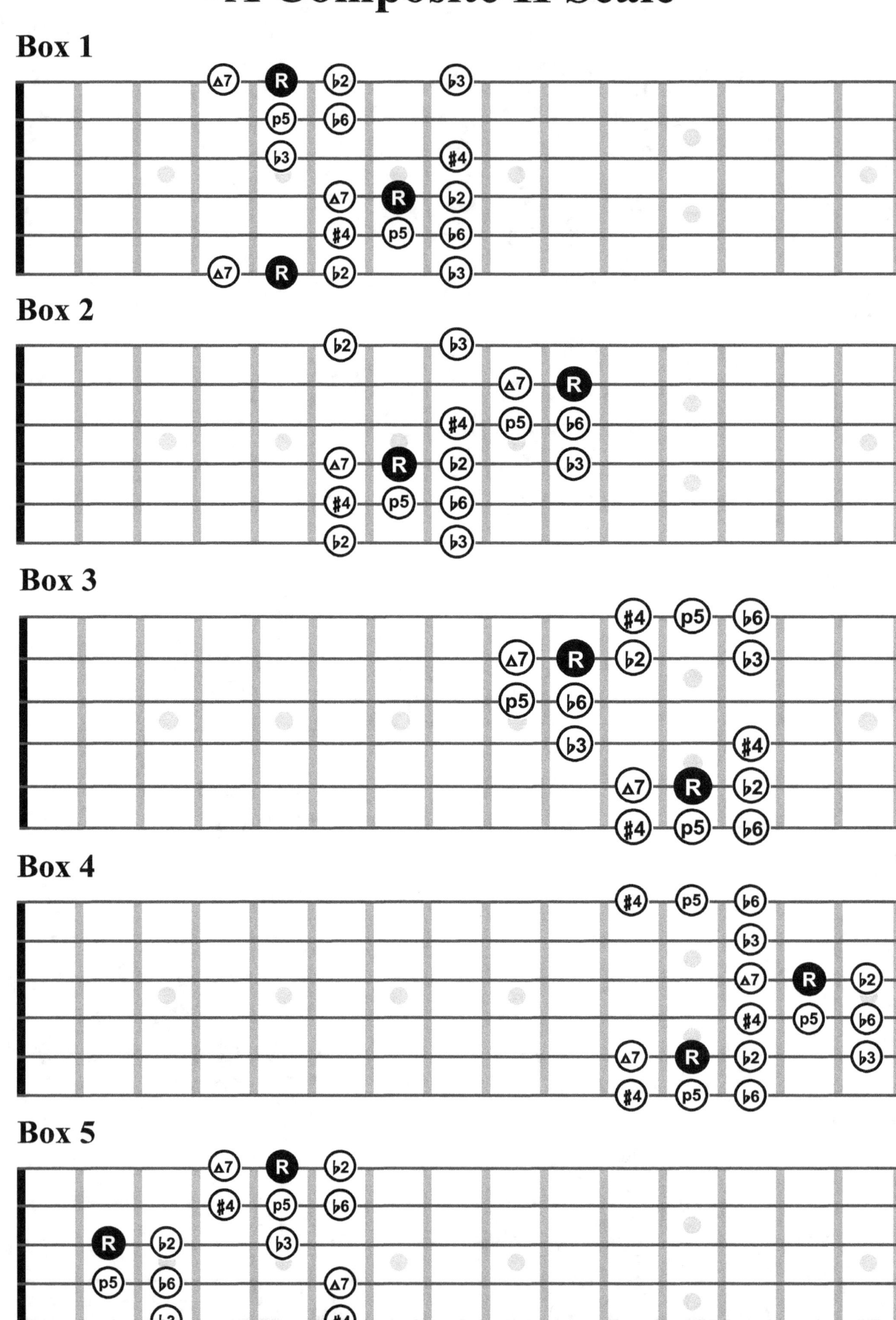

Box 1

Box 2

Box 3

Box 4

Box 5

A Prometheus Scale

Box 1

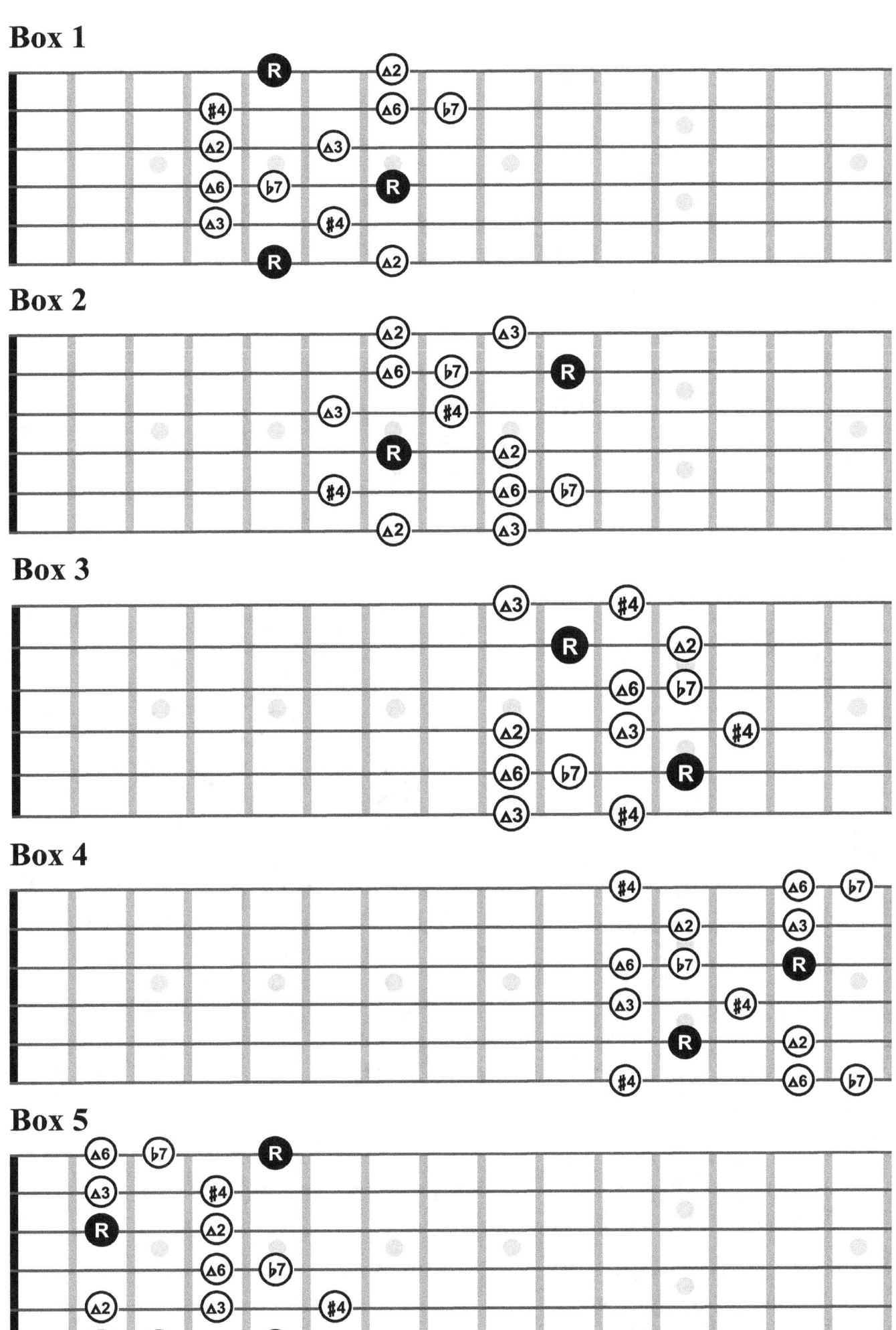

Box 2

Box 3

Box 4

Box 5

A Prometheus Neapolitan Scale

Box 1

Box 2

Box 3

Box 4

Box 5

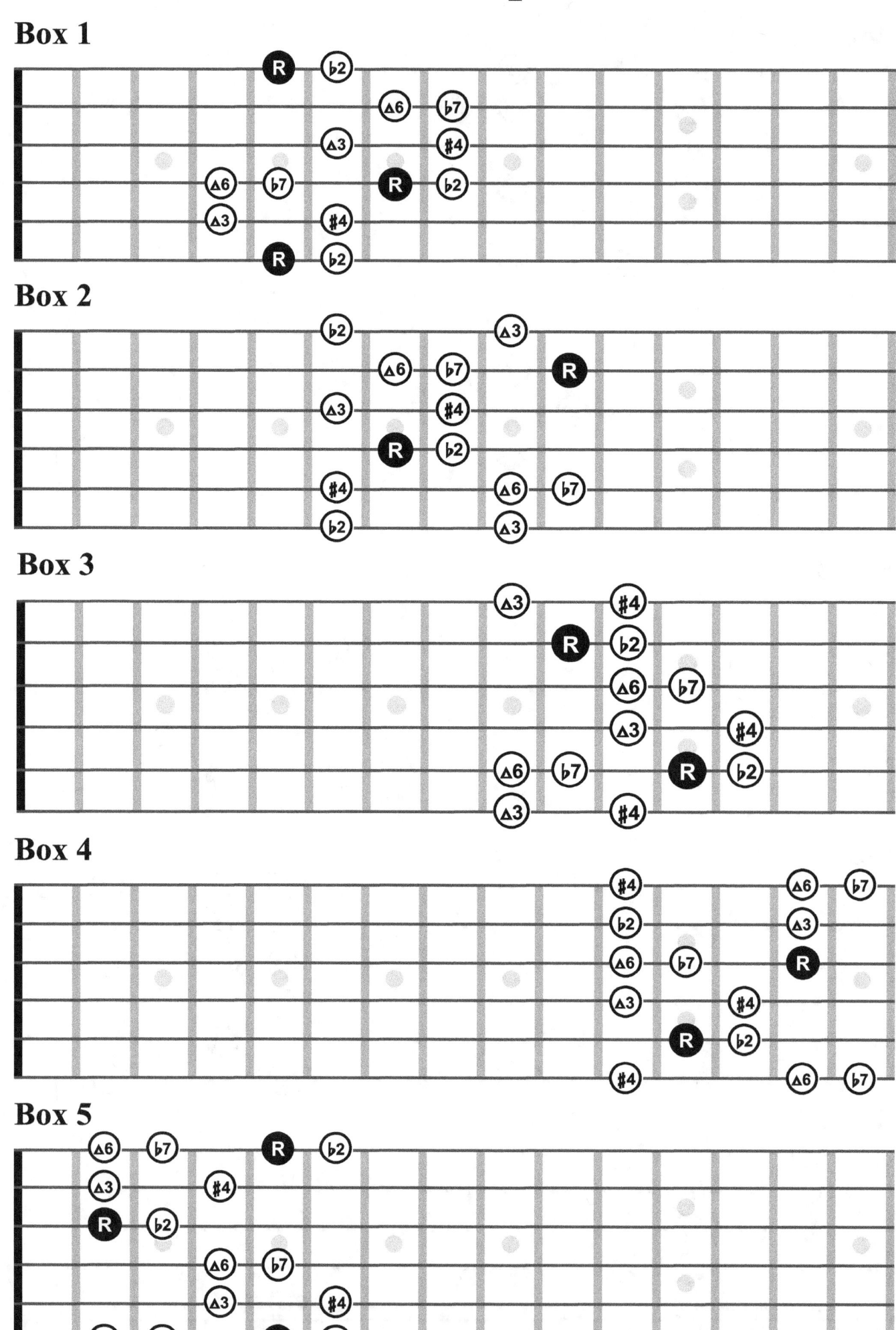

A Scriabin Scale

Box 1

Box 2

Box 3

Box 4

Box 5

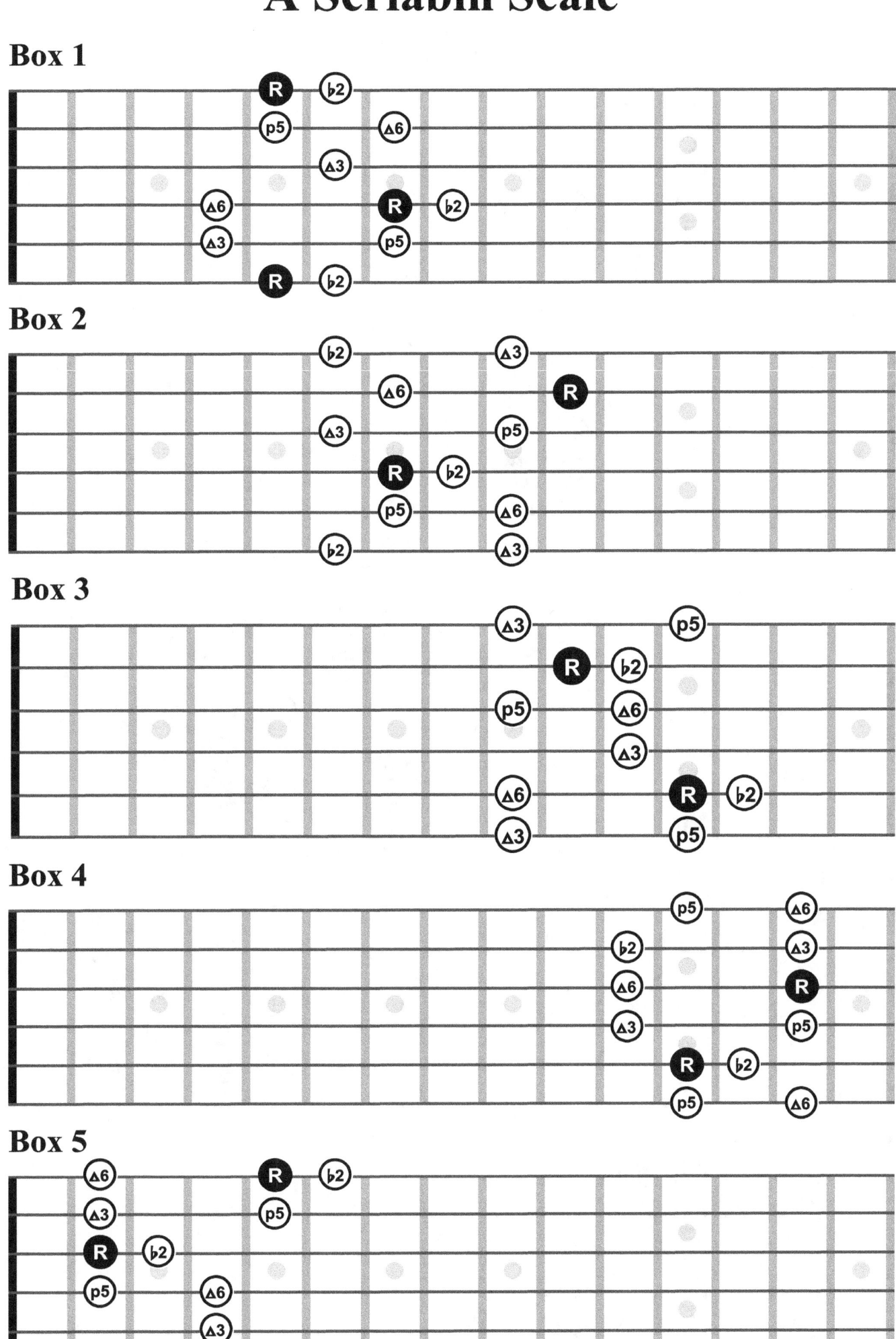

A Ionian b5 Scale

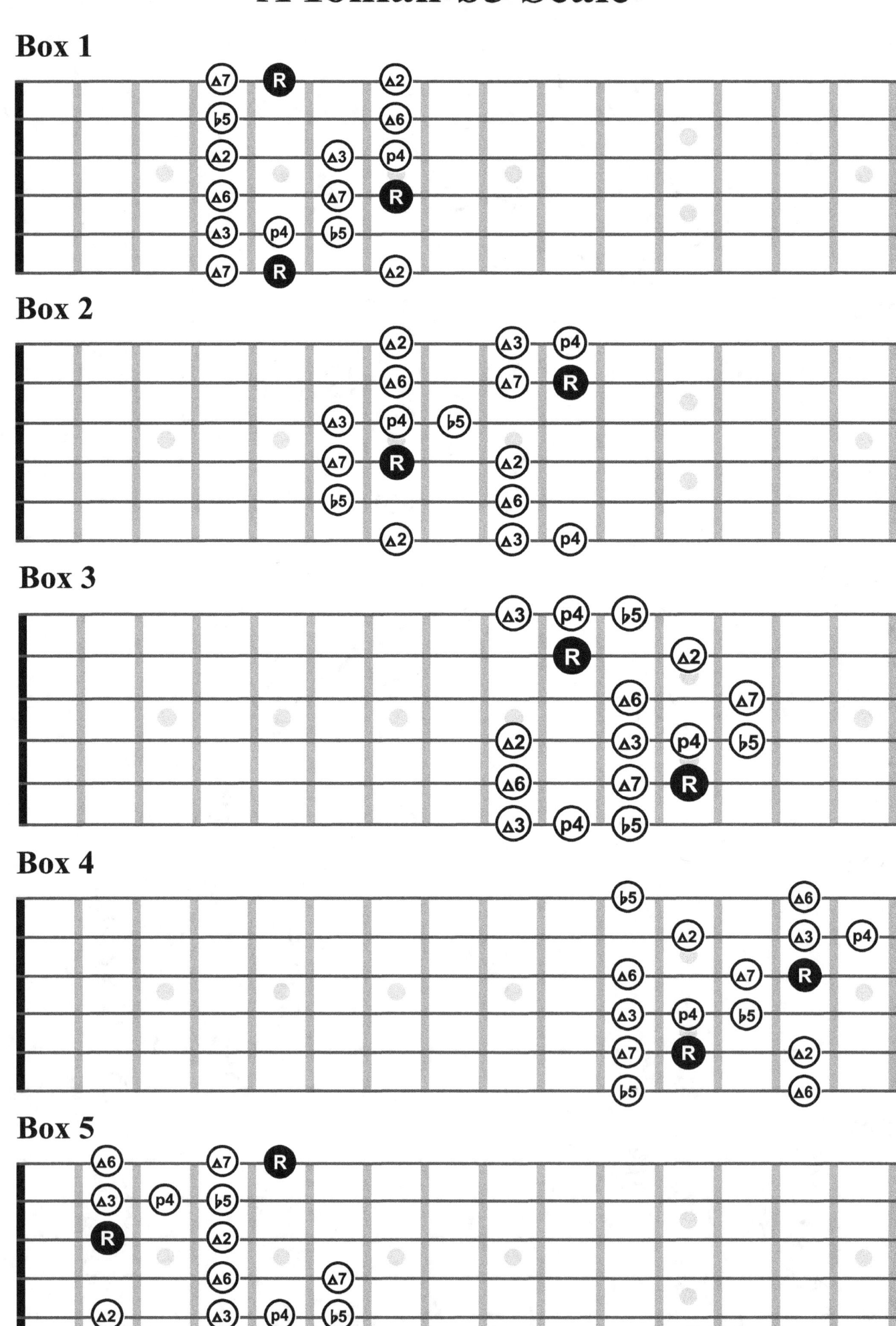

A Locrian Natural 7 Scale

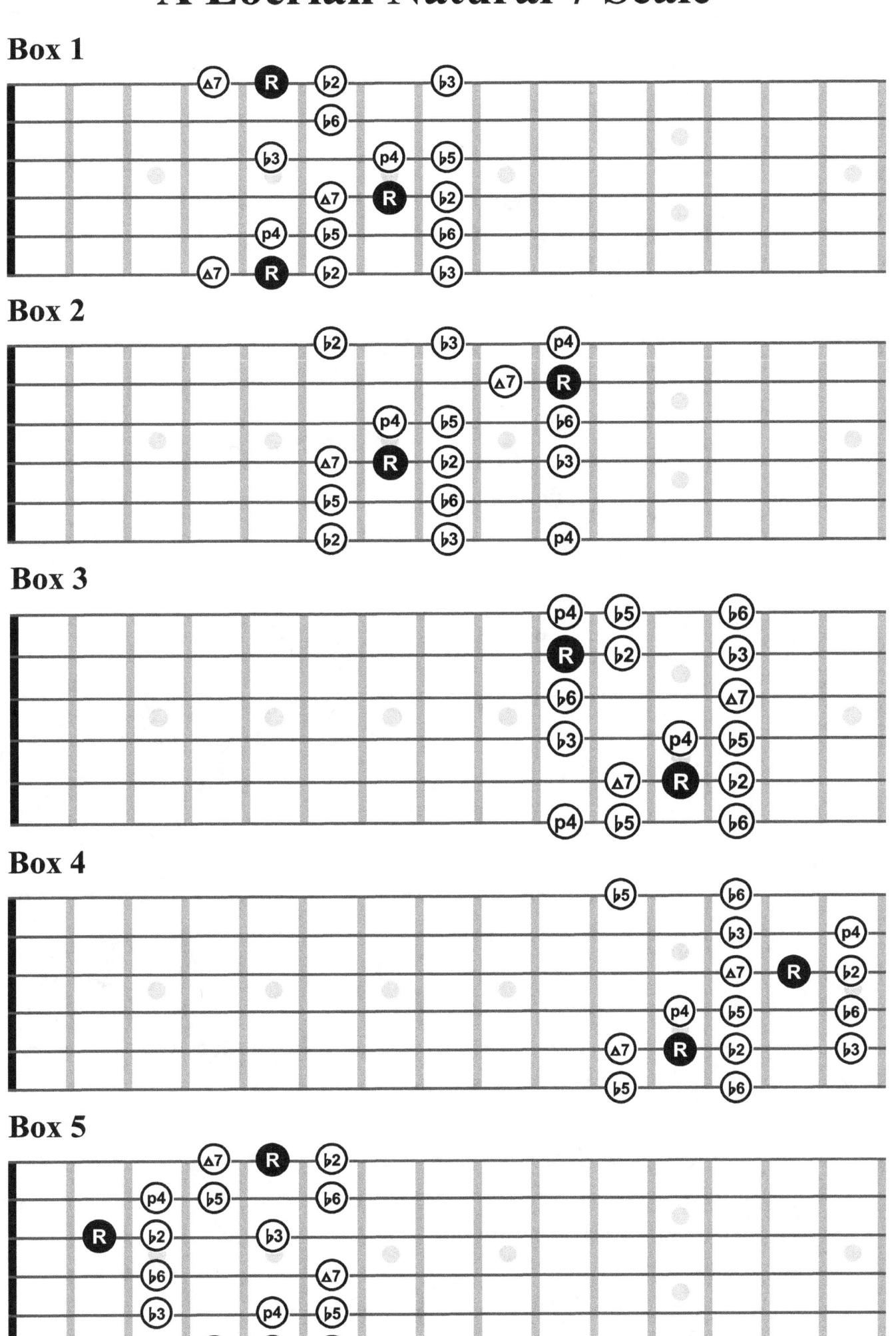

A Persian Scale

Box 1

Box 2

Box 3

Box 4

Box 5

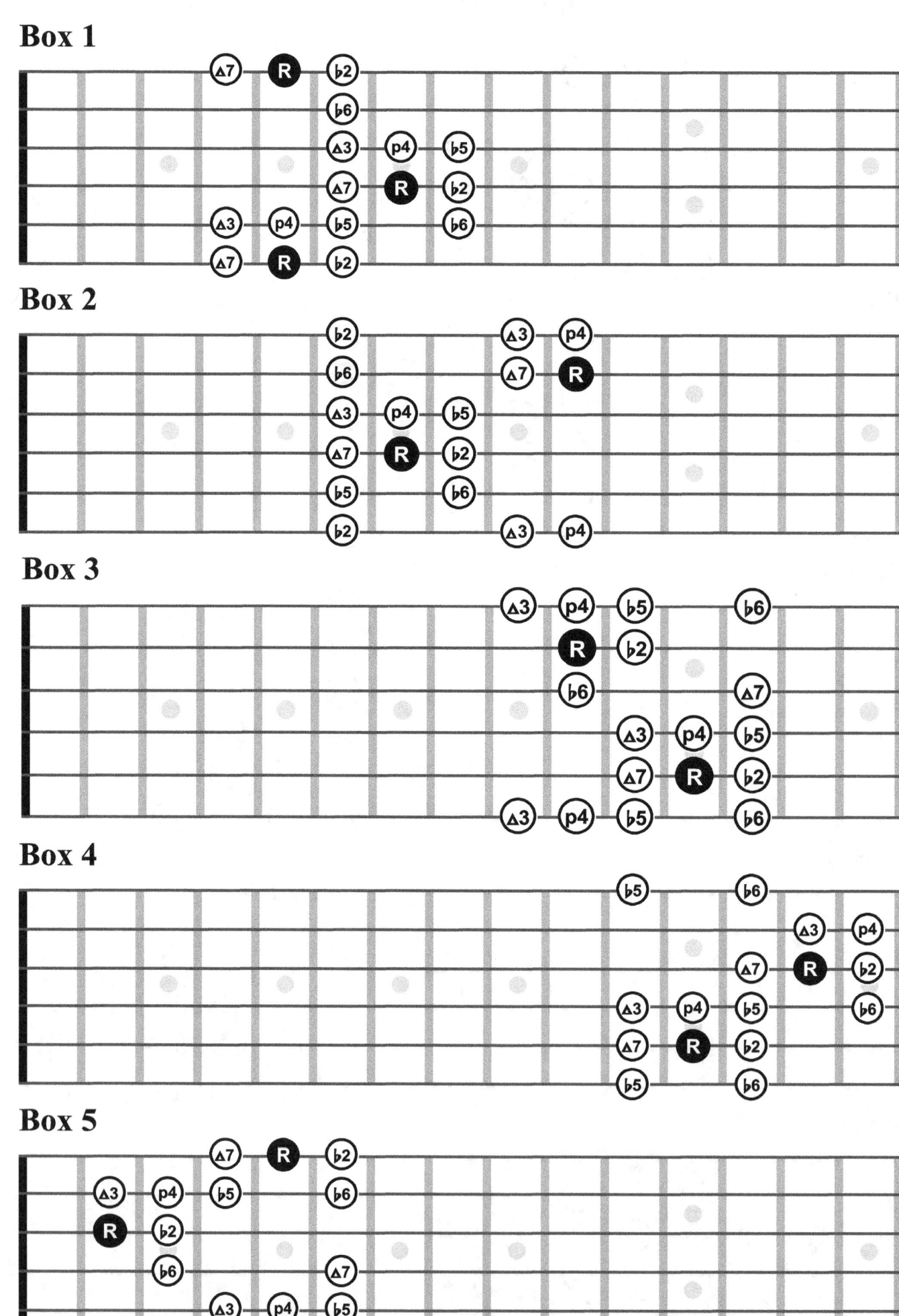

A Balinese Scale

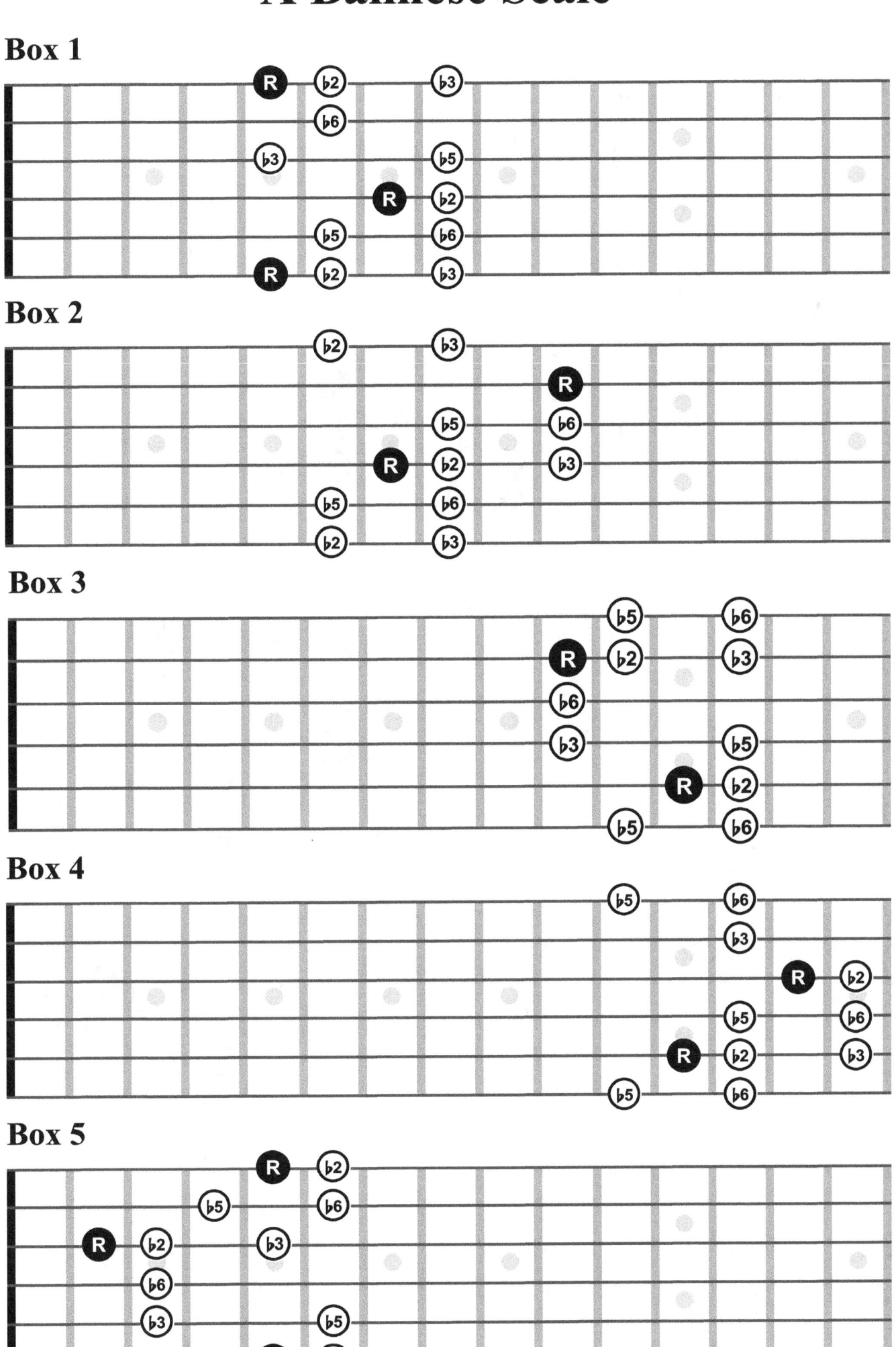

Box 1

Box 2

Box 3

Box 4

Box 5

A Pelog Scale

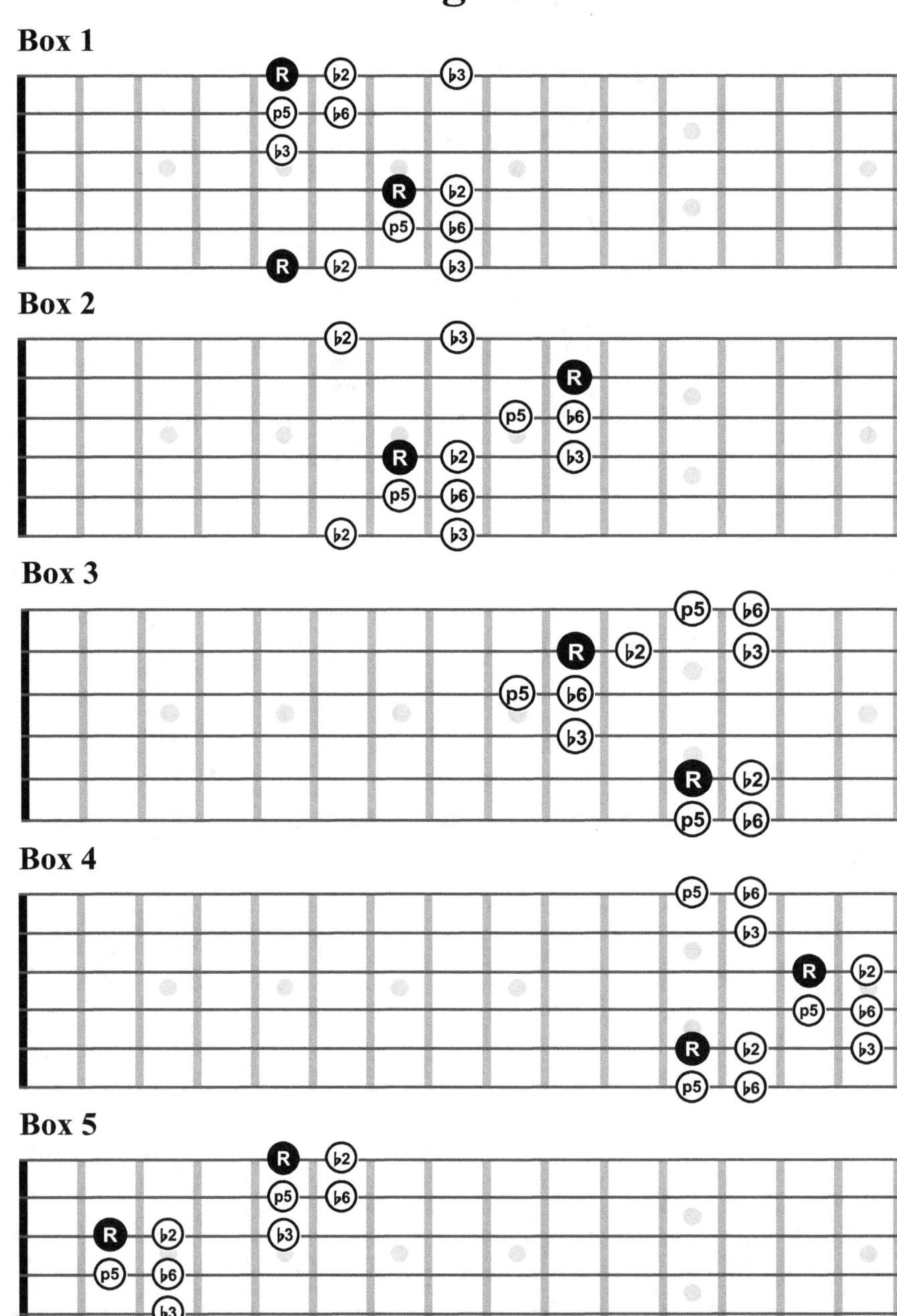

A Algerian Scale

Box 1

Box 2

Box 3

Box 4

Box 5

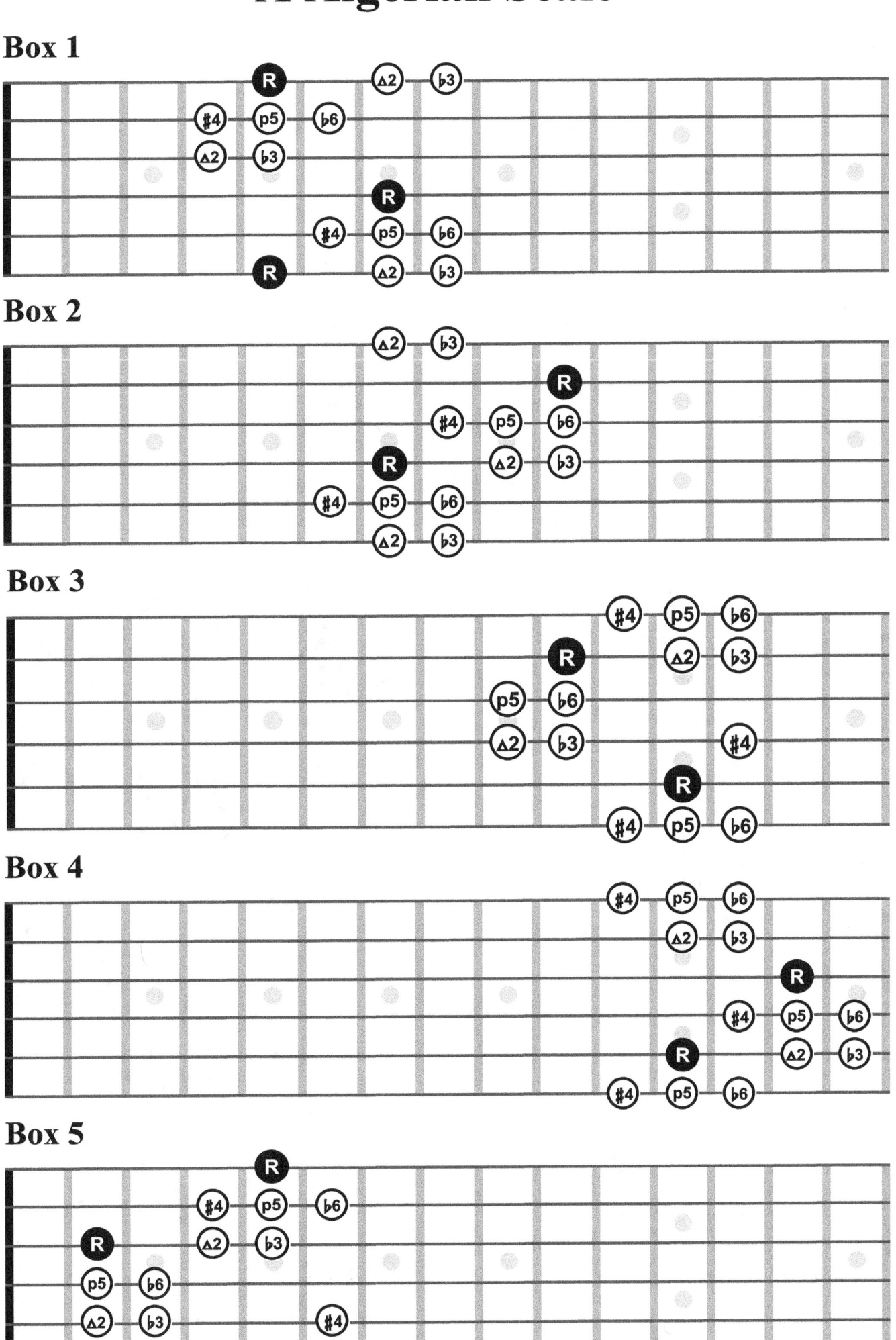

A Japanese Scale

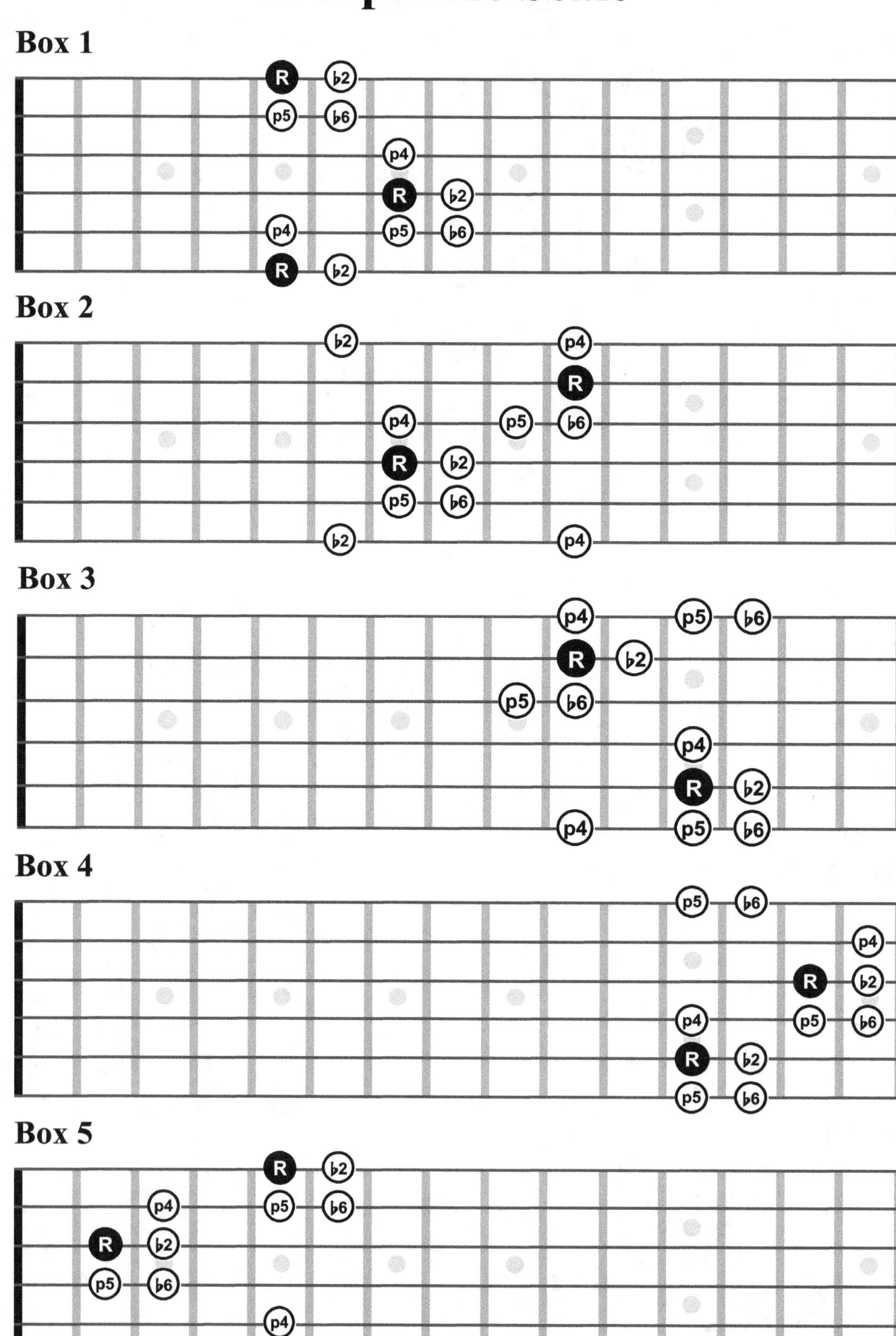

Box 1

Box 2

Box 3

Box 4

Box 5

A Hirajoshi Scale

Box 1

Box 2

Box 3

Box 4

Box 5

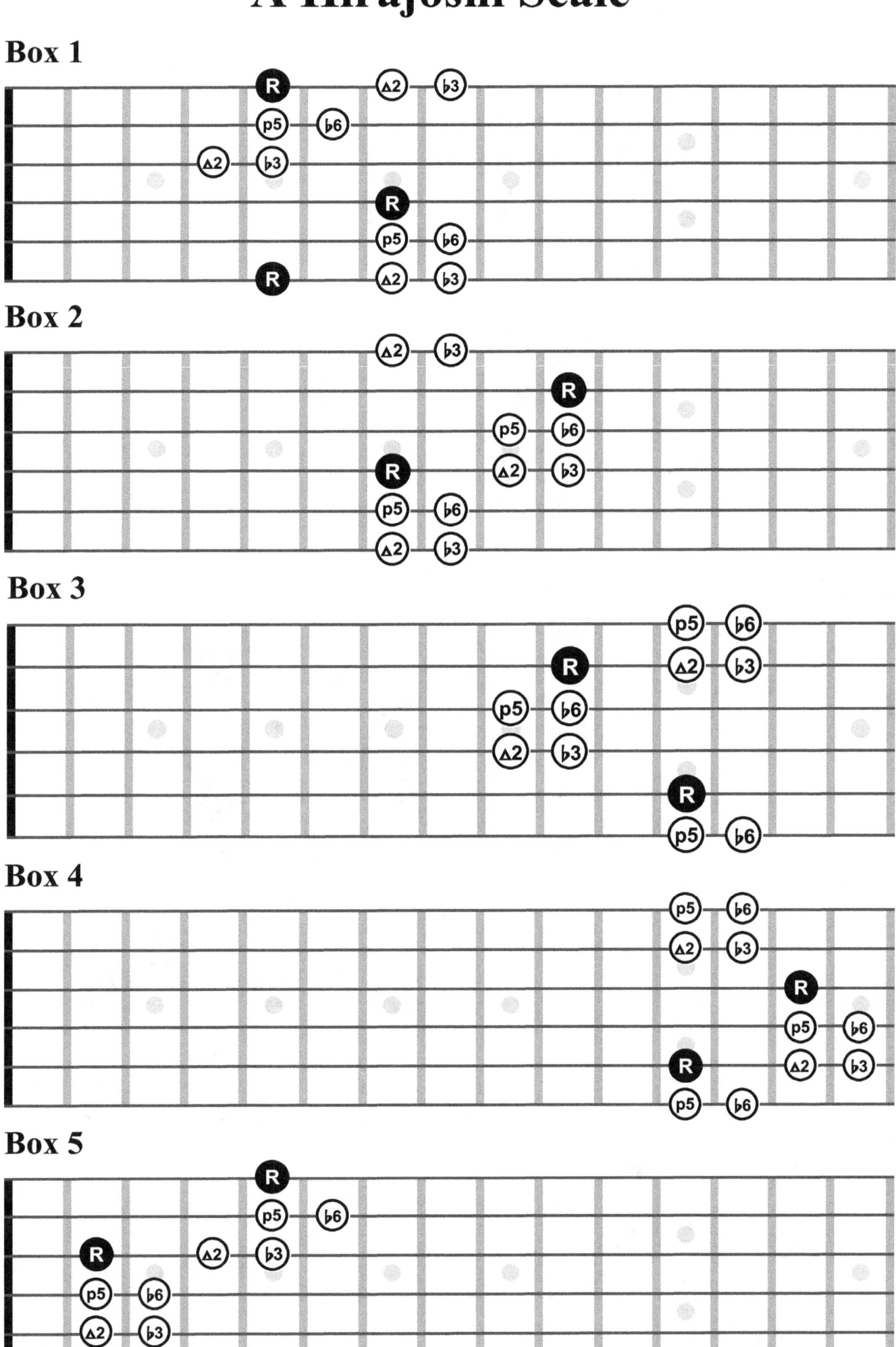

A Kumoi Scale

Box 1

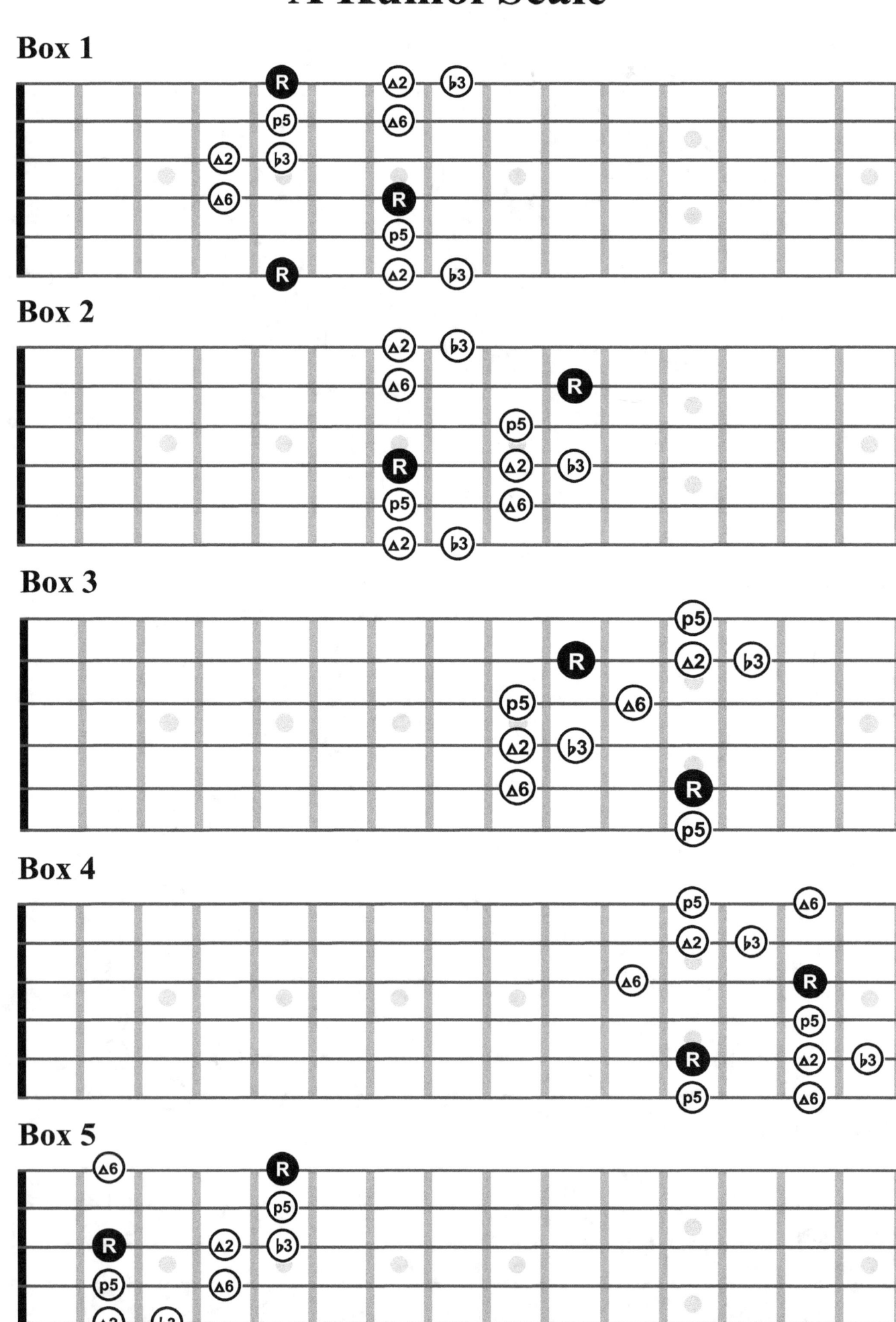

Box 2

Box 3

Box 4

Box 5

A Iwato Scale

Box 1

Box 2

Box 3

Box 4

Box 5

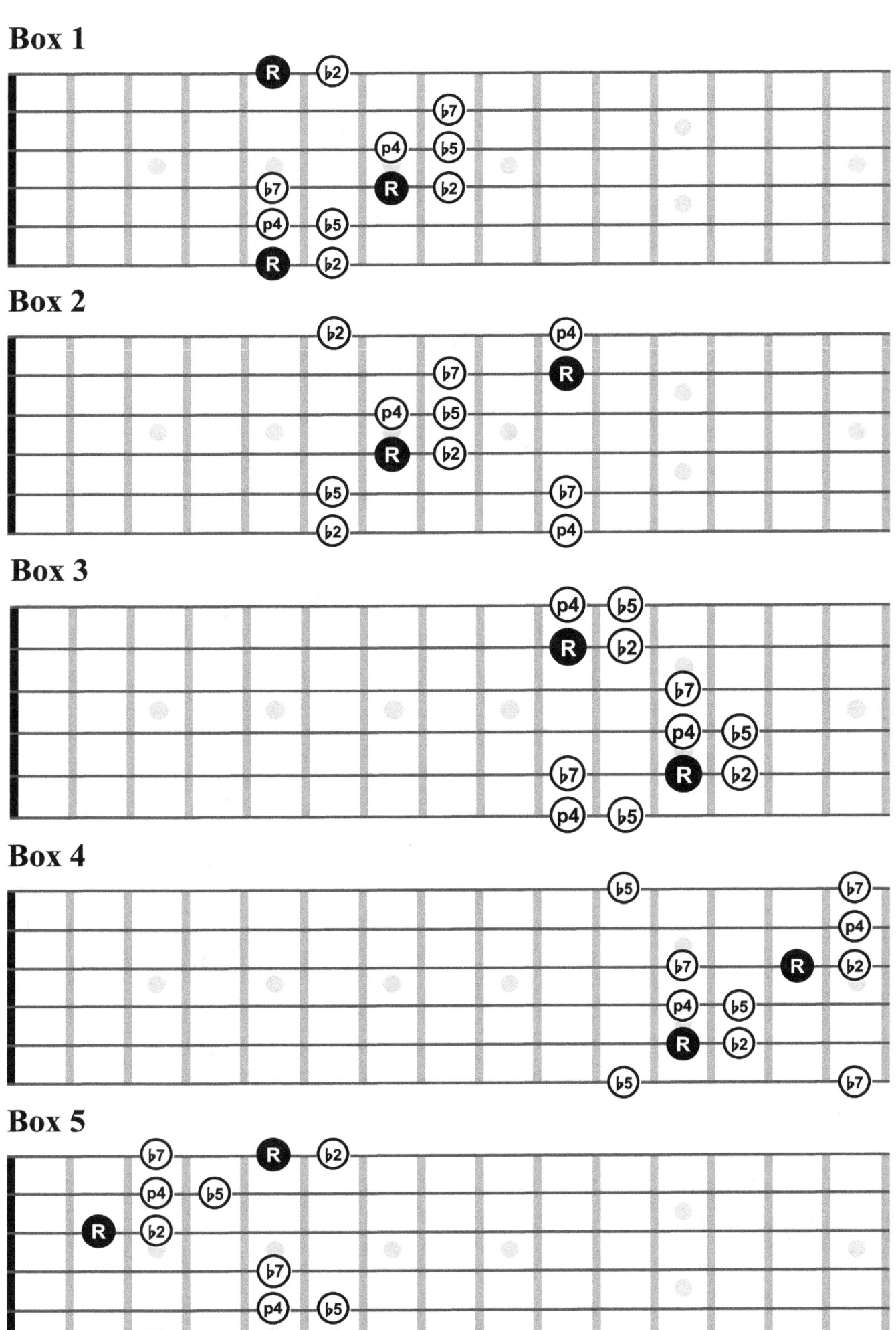

A In-Sen Scale

Box 1

Box 2

Box 3

Box 4

Box 5

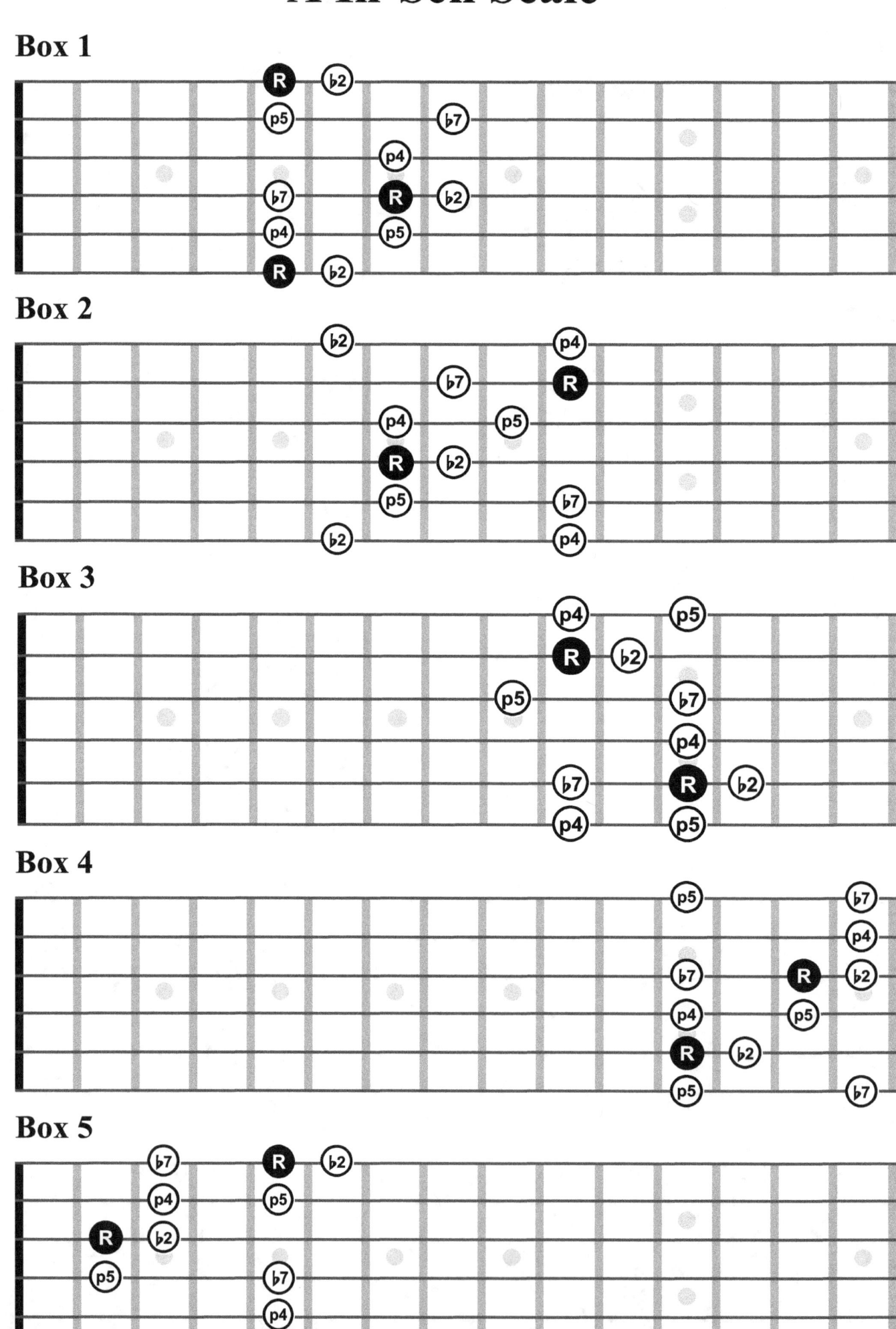

A Chinese Scale

Box 1

Box 2

Box 3

Box 4

Box 5

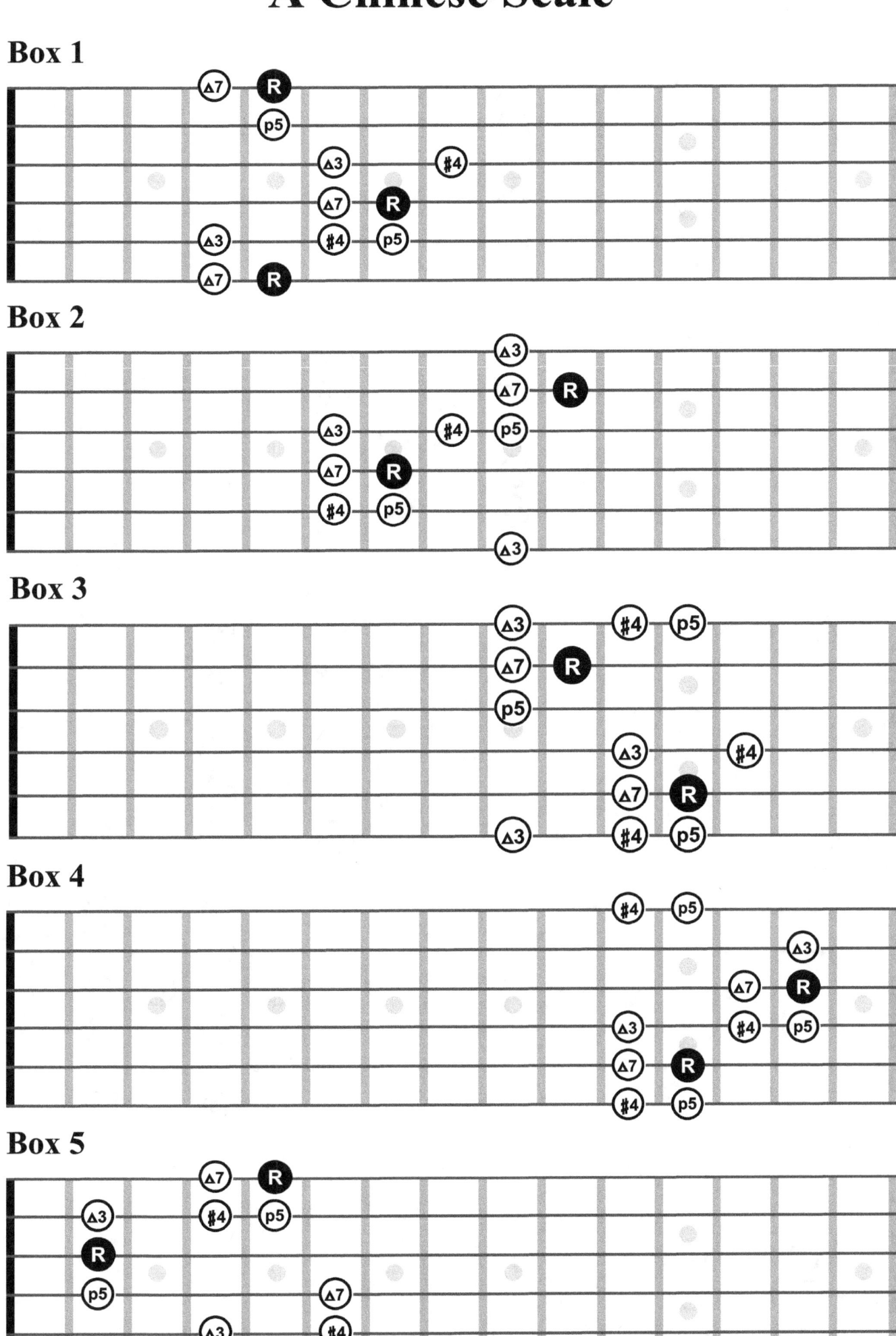

A P'yongio Scale

Box 1

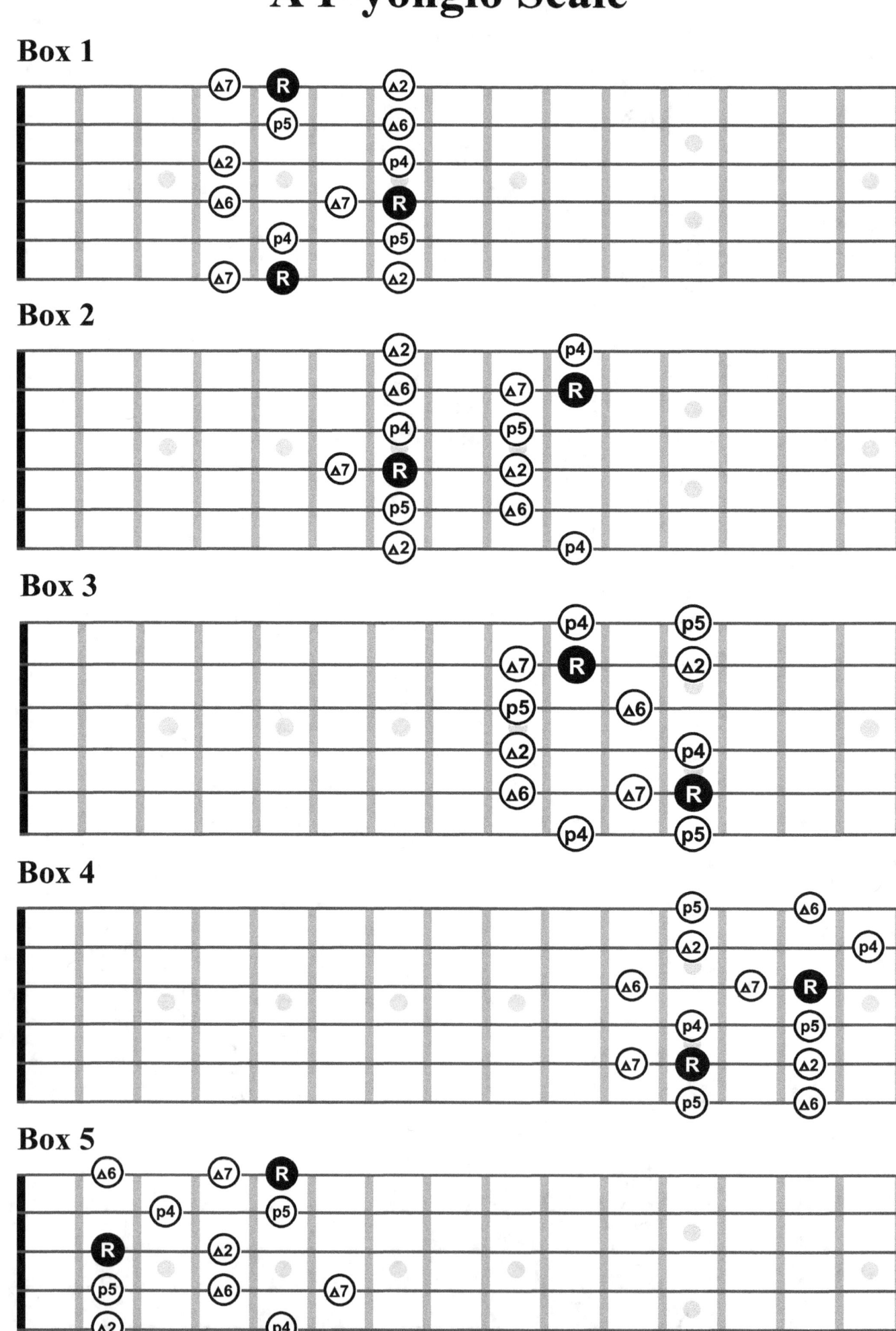

Box 2

Box 3

Box 4

Box 5

A Dominant Sus Scale

Box 1

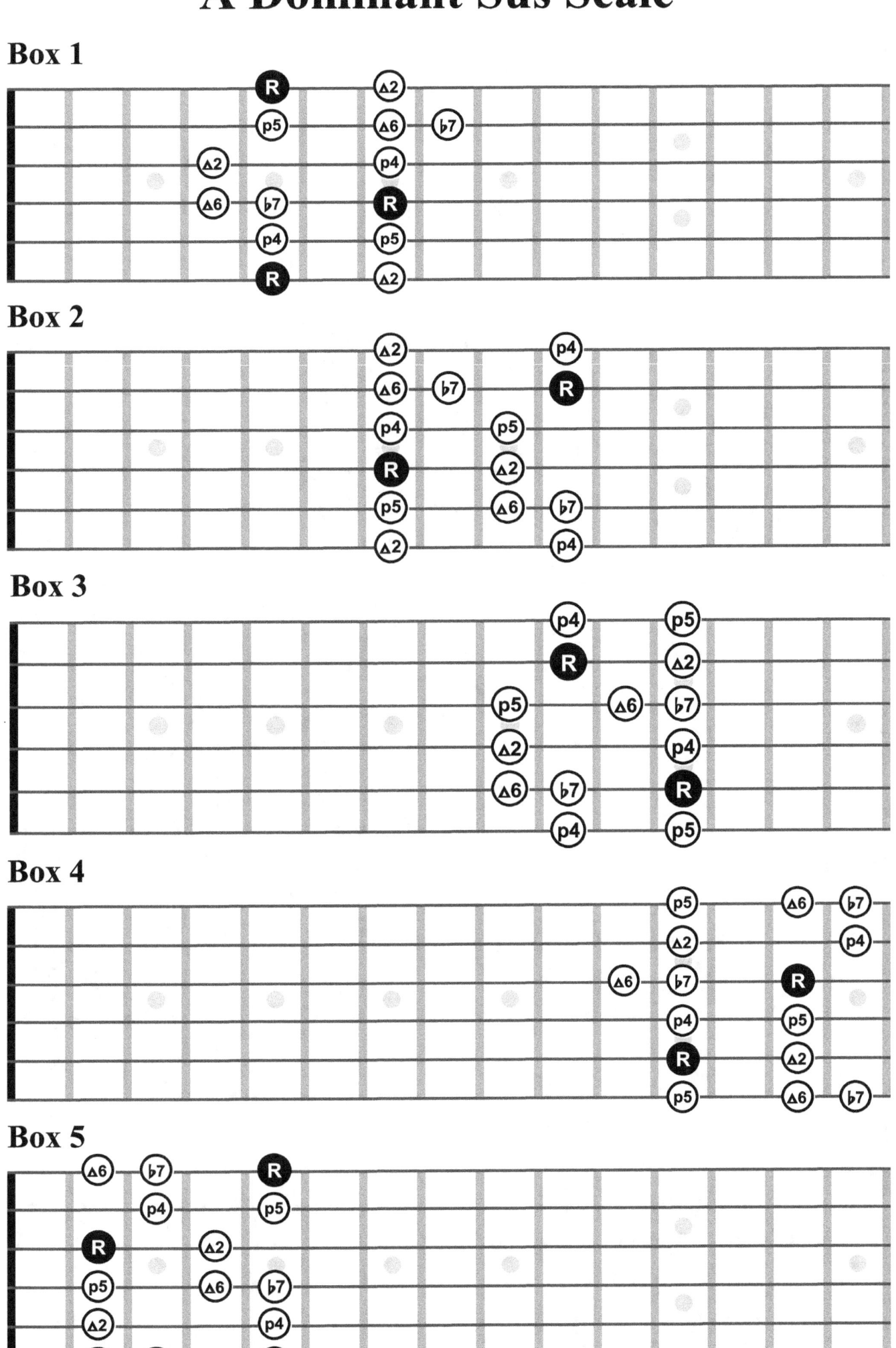

Box 2

Box 3

Box 4

Box 5

A 8-Tone Spanish Scale

Box 1

Box 2

Box 3

Box 4

Box 5

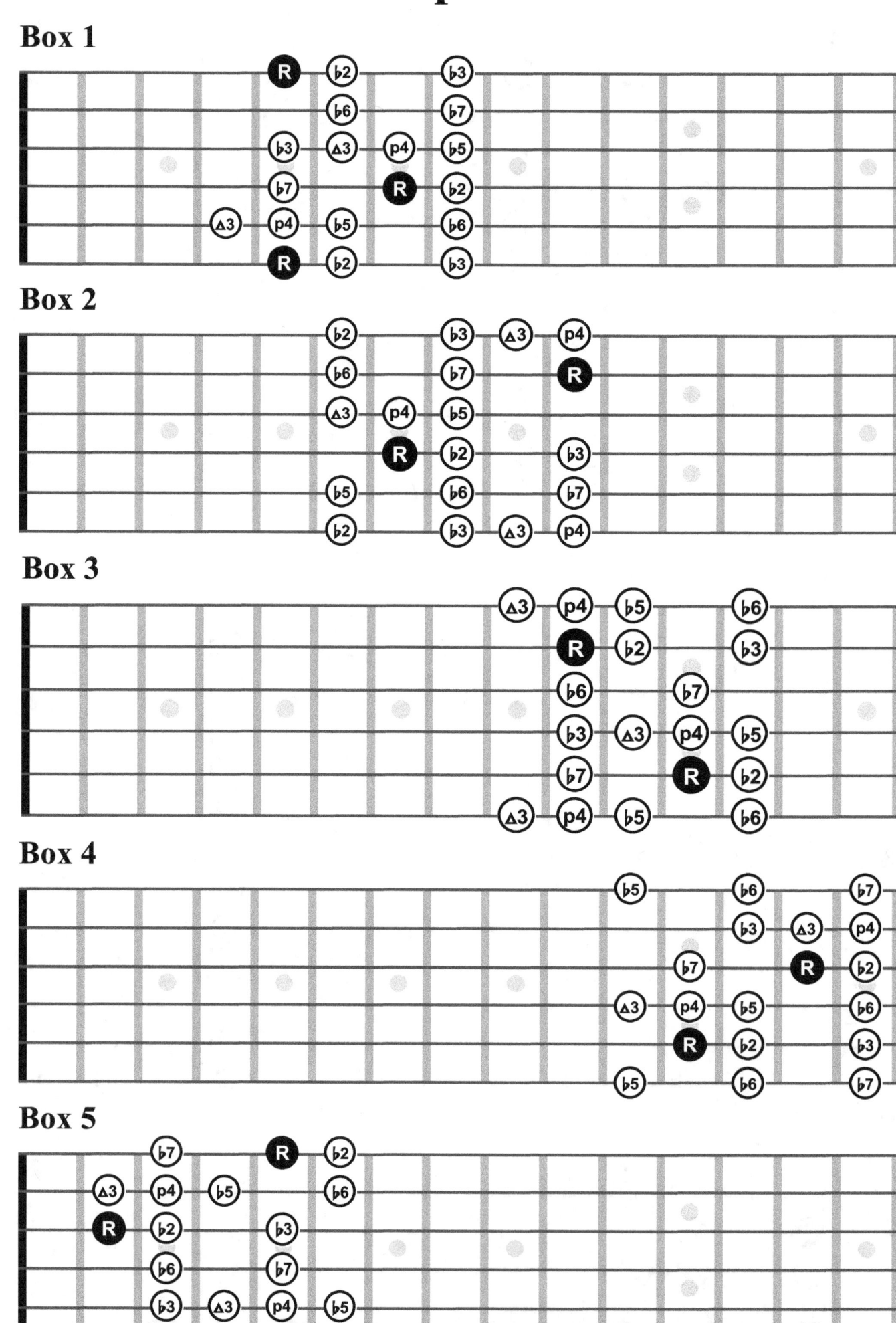

A Bebop Major Scale

Box 1

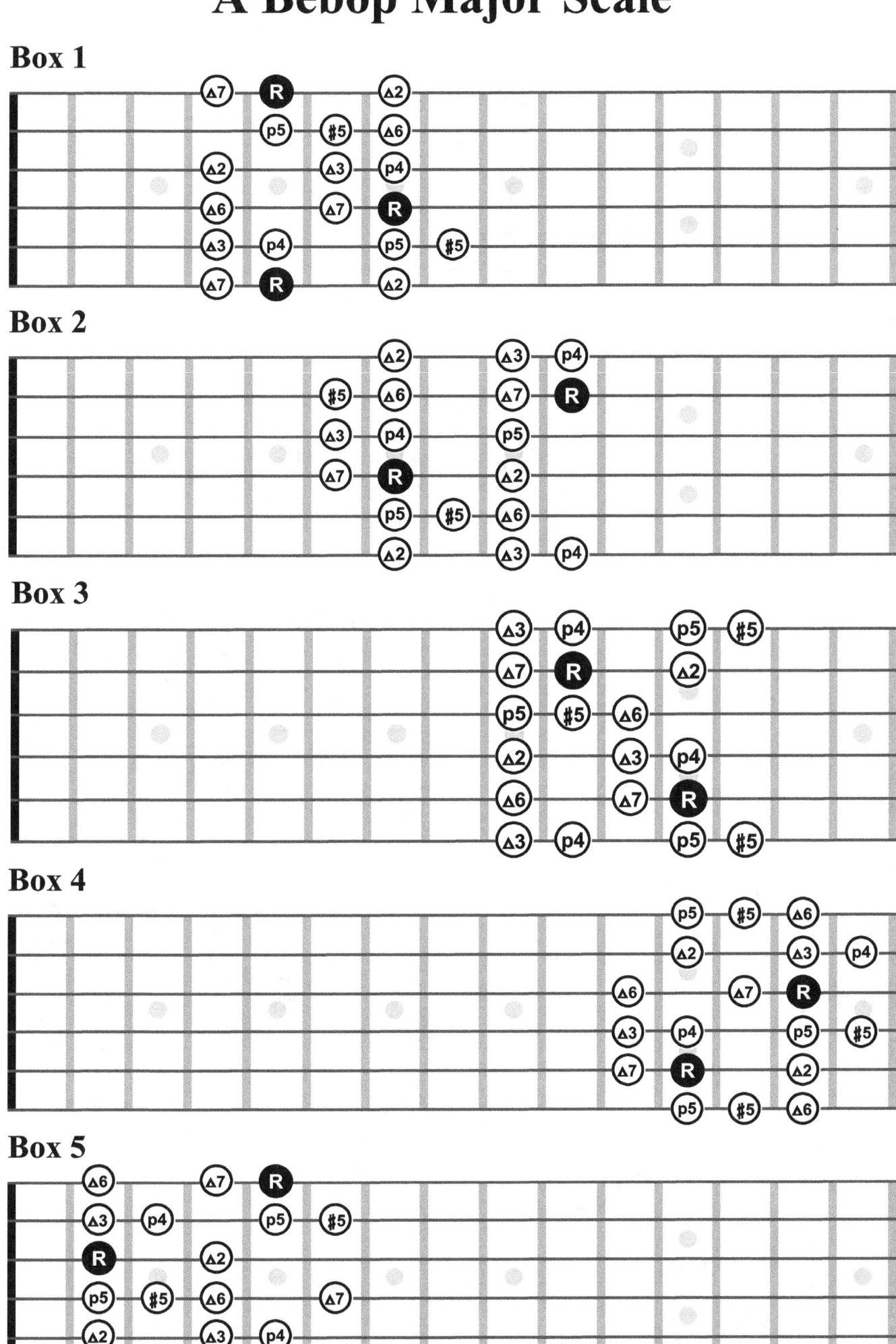

Box 2

Box 3

Box 4

Box 5

A Bebop Minor Scale

Box 1

Box 2

Box 3

Box 4

Box 5

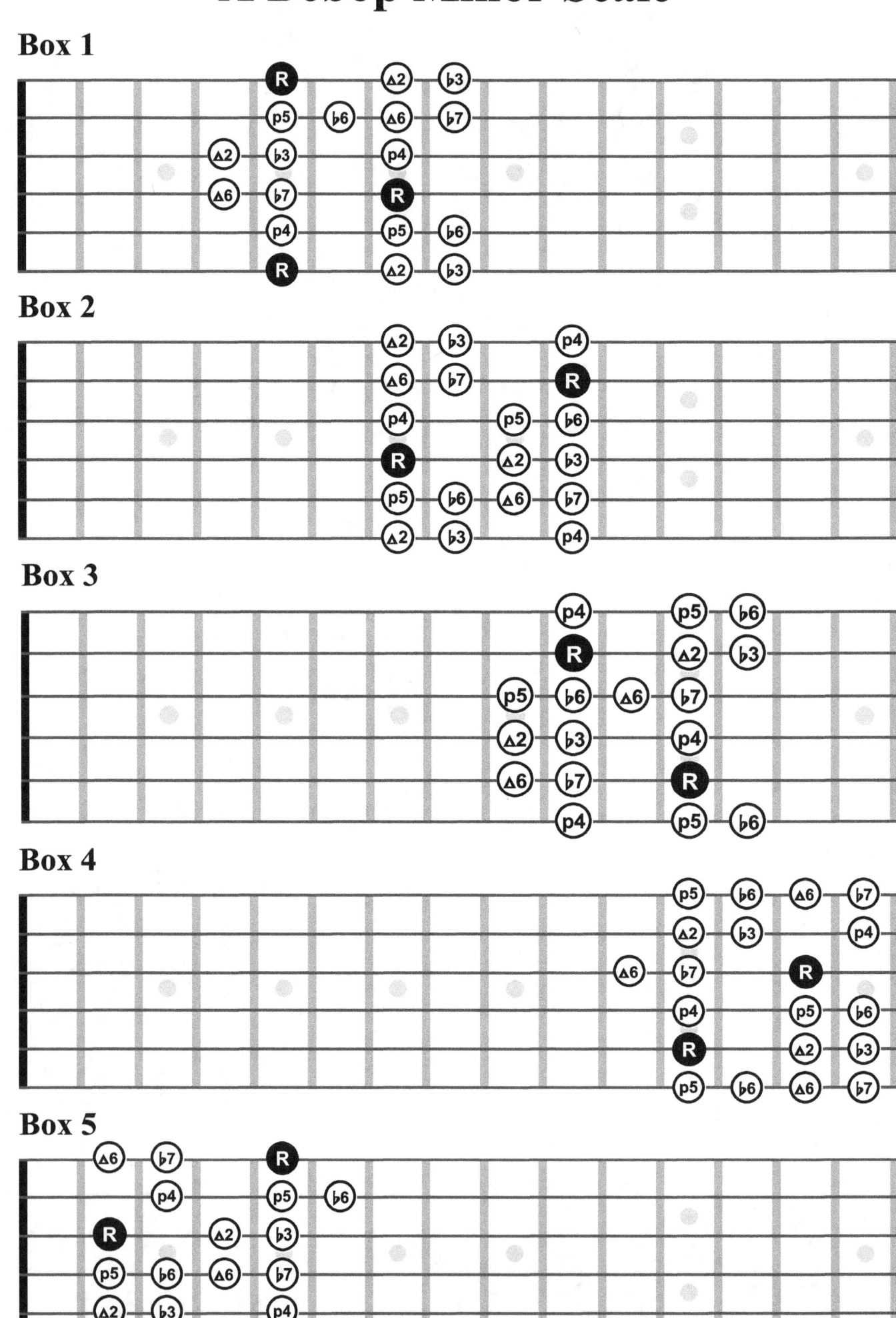

A Bebop Dominant Scale

Box 1

Box 2

Box 3

Box 4

Box 5

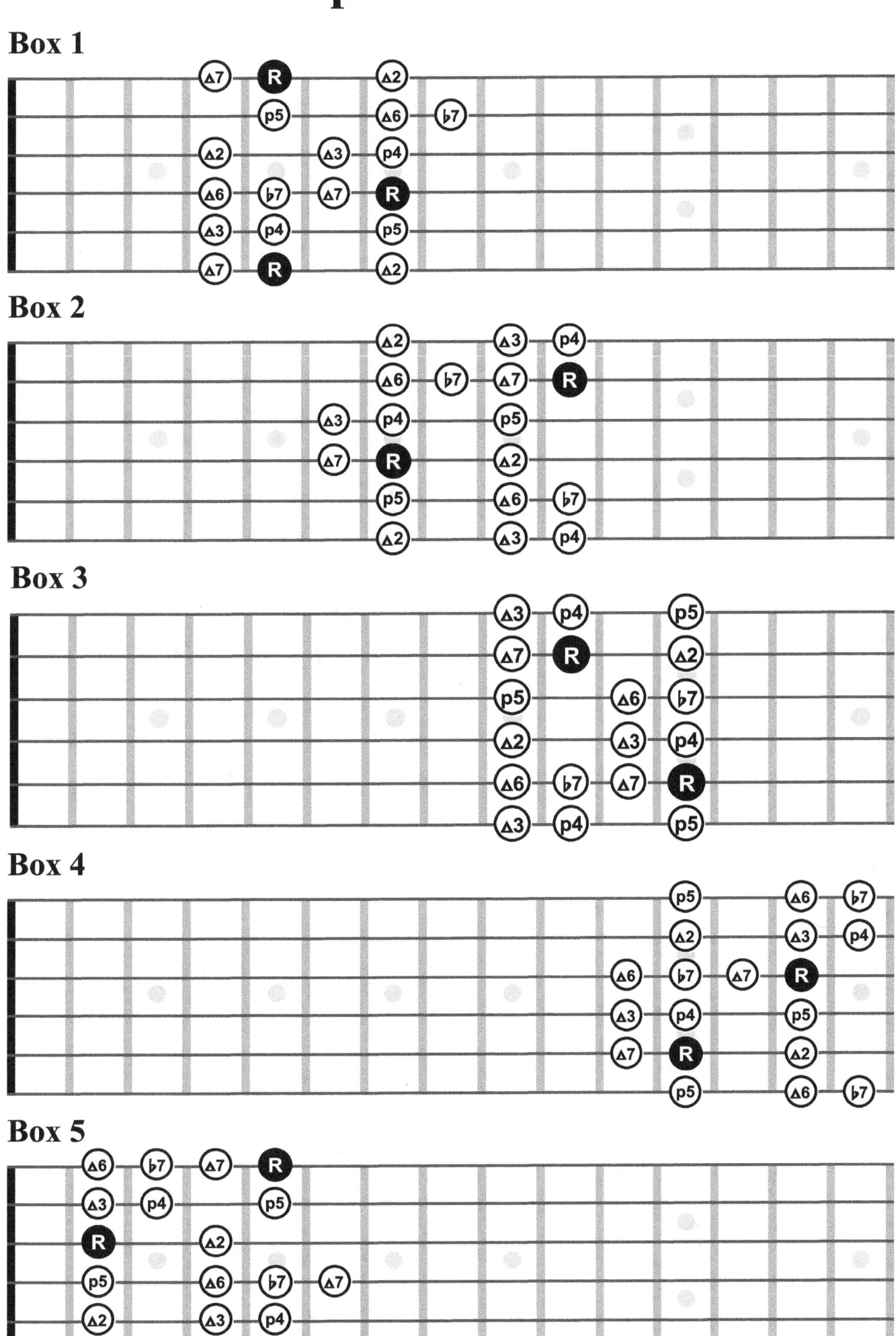

A Bebop Dorian Scale

Box 1

Box 2

Box 3

Box 4

Box 5

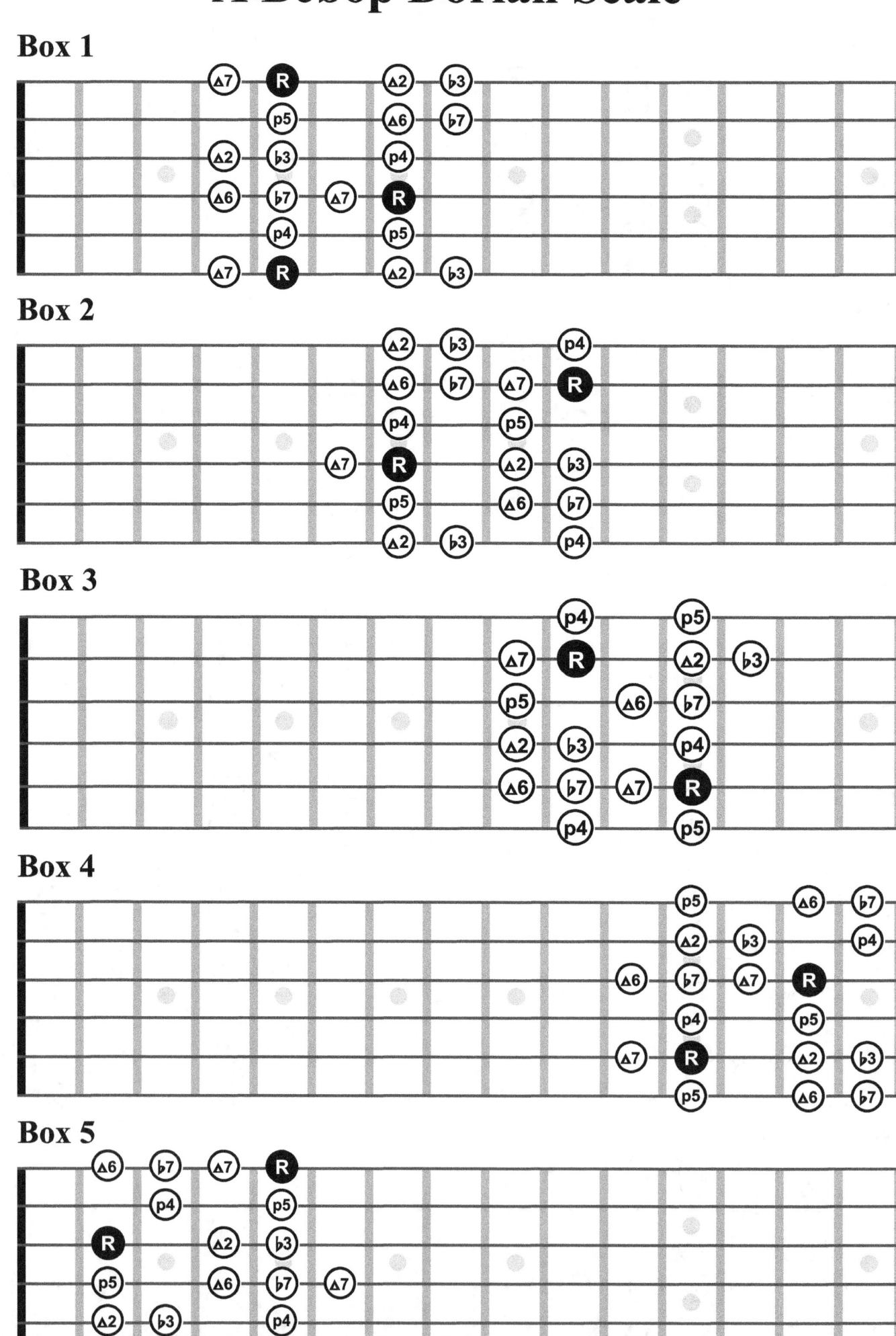

A Bebop Locrian add 5 Scale

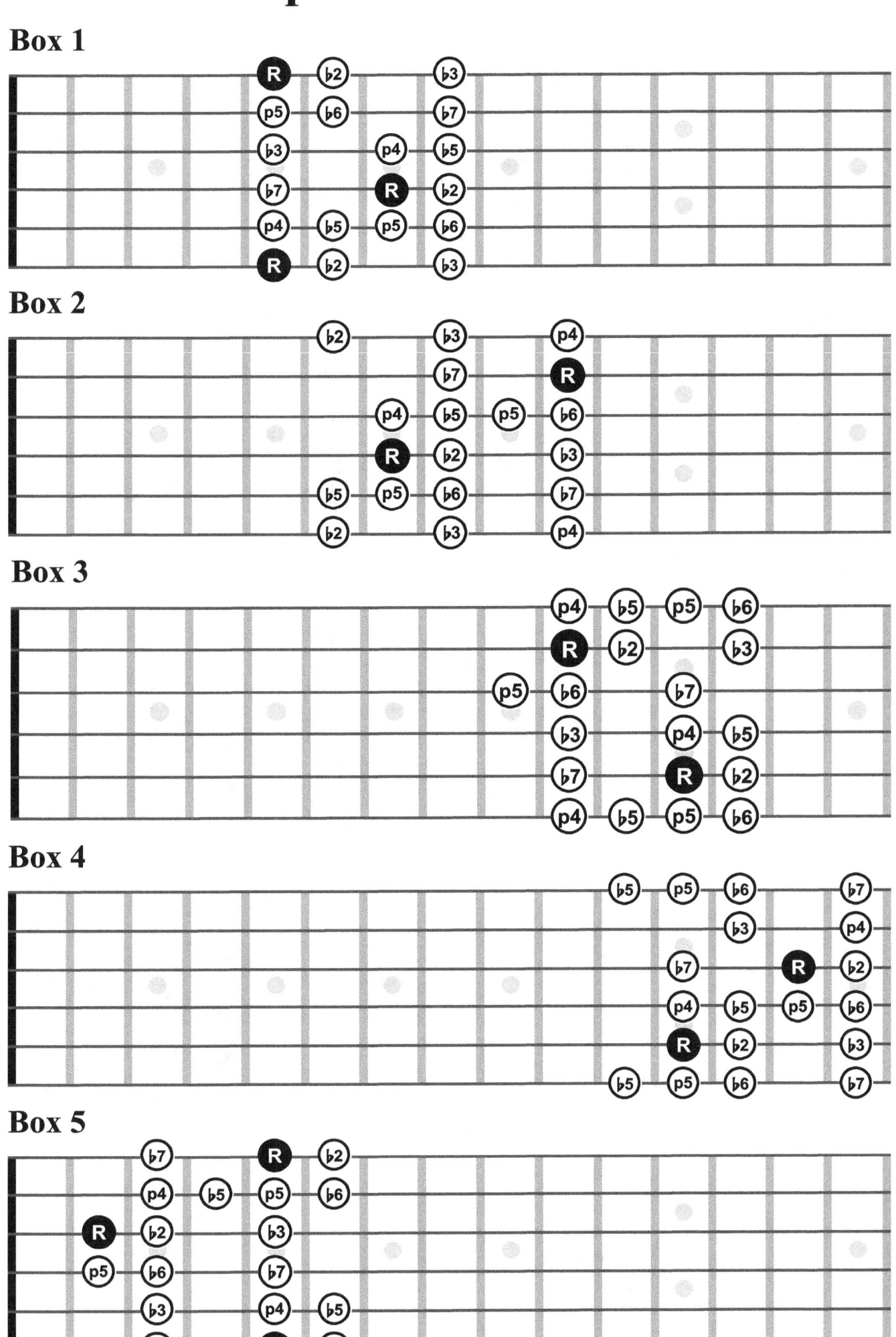

A Bebop Locrian Natural 2 Scale

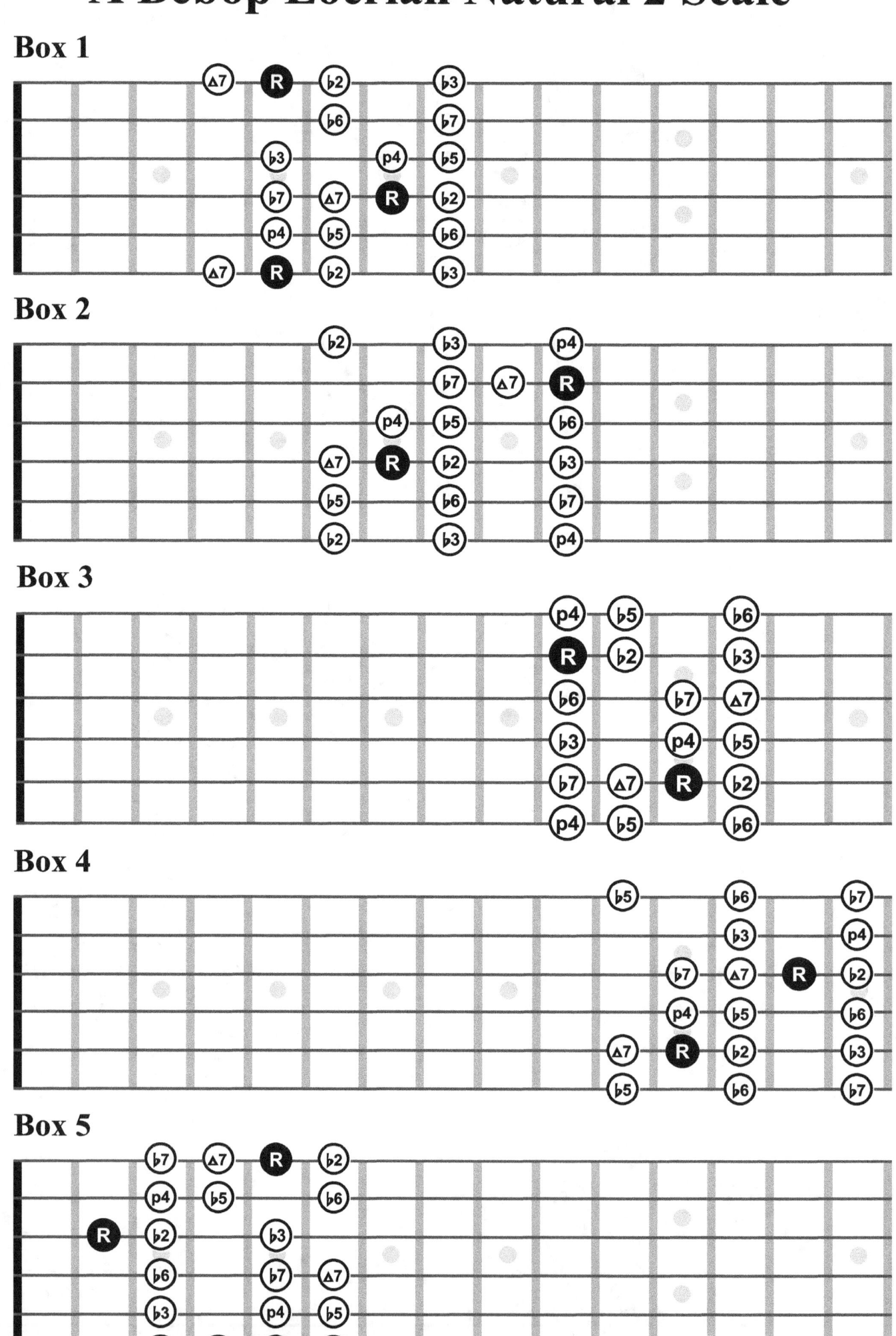

Box 1

Box 2

Box 3

Box 4

Box 5

A Ionian Scale

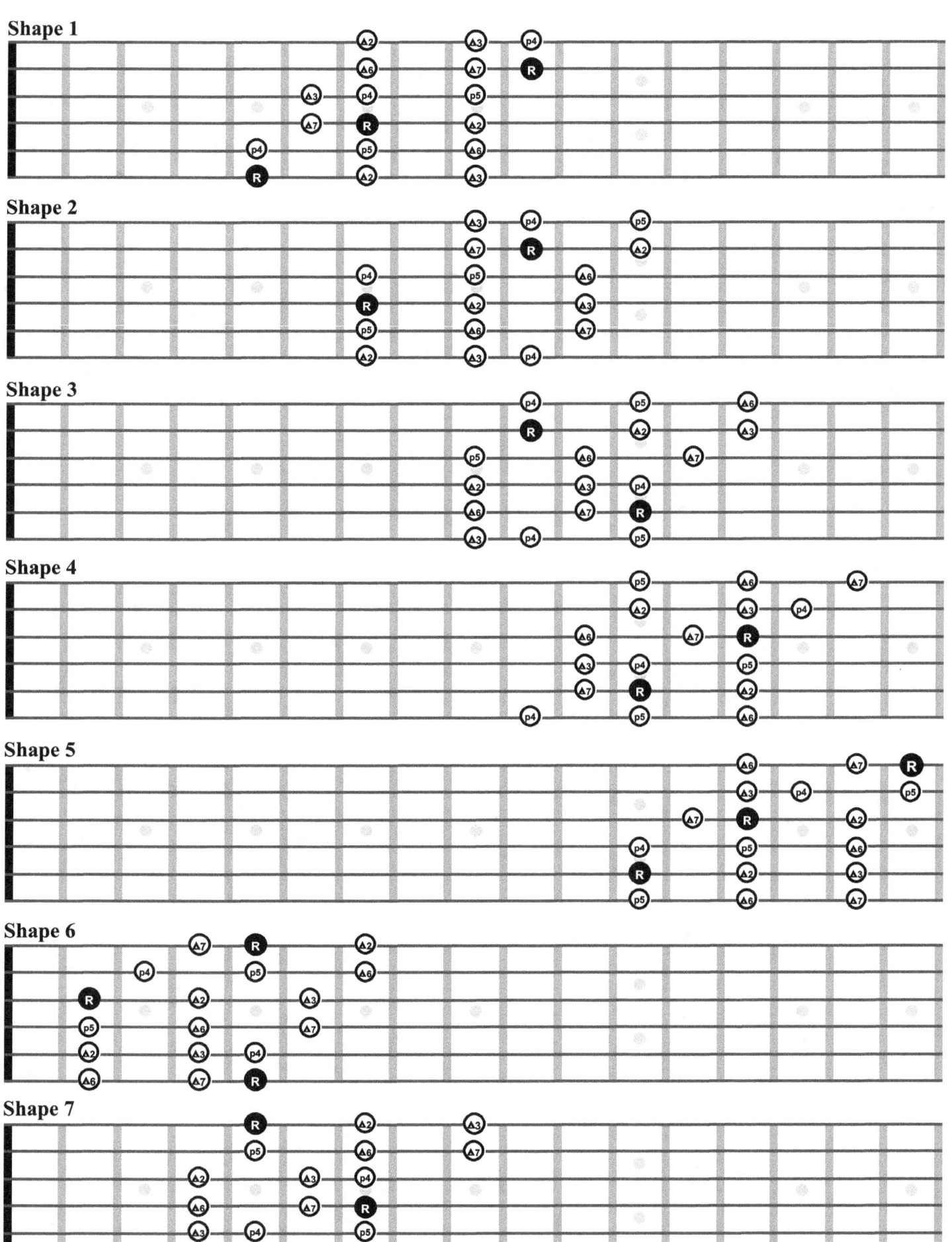

A Dorian Scale

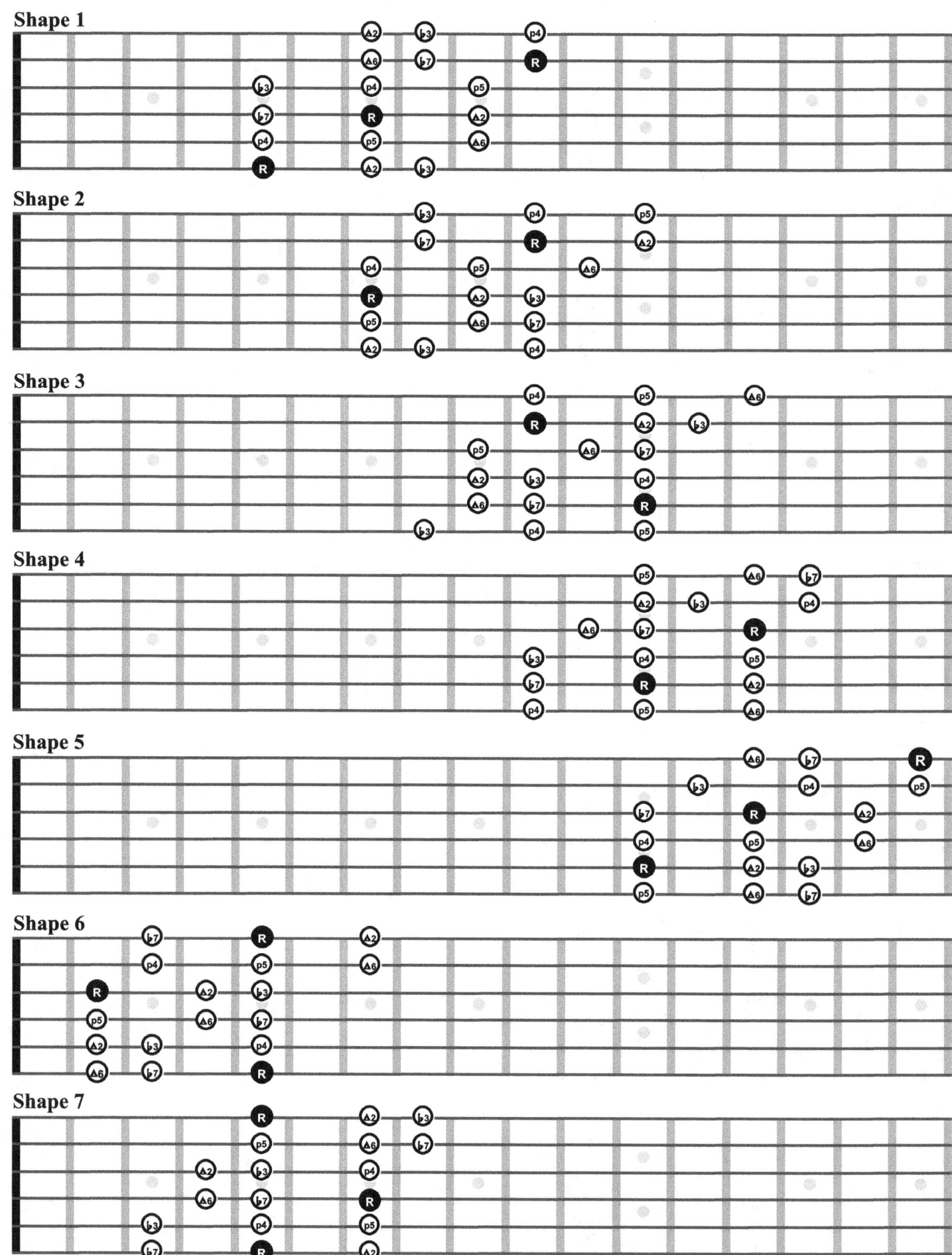

A Phrygian Scale

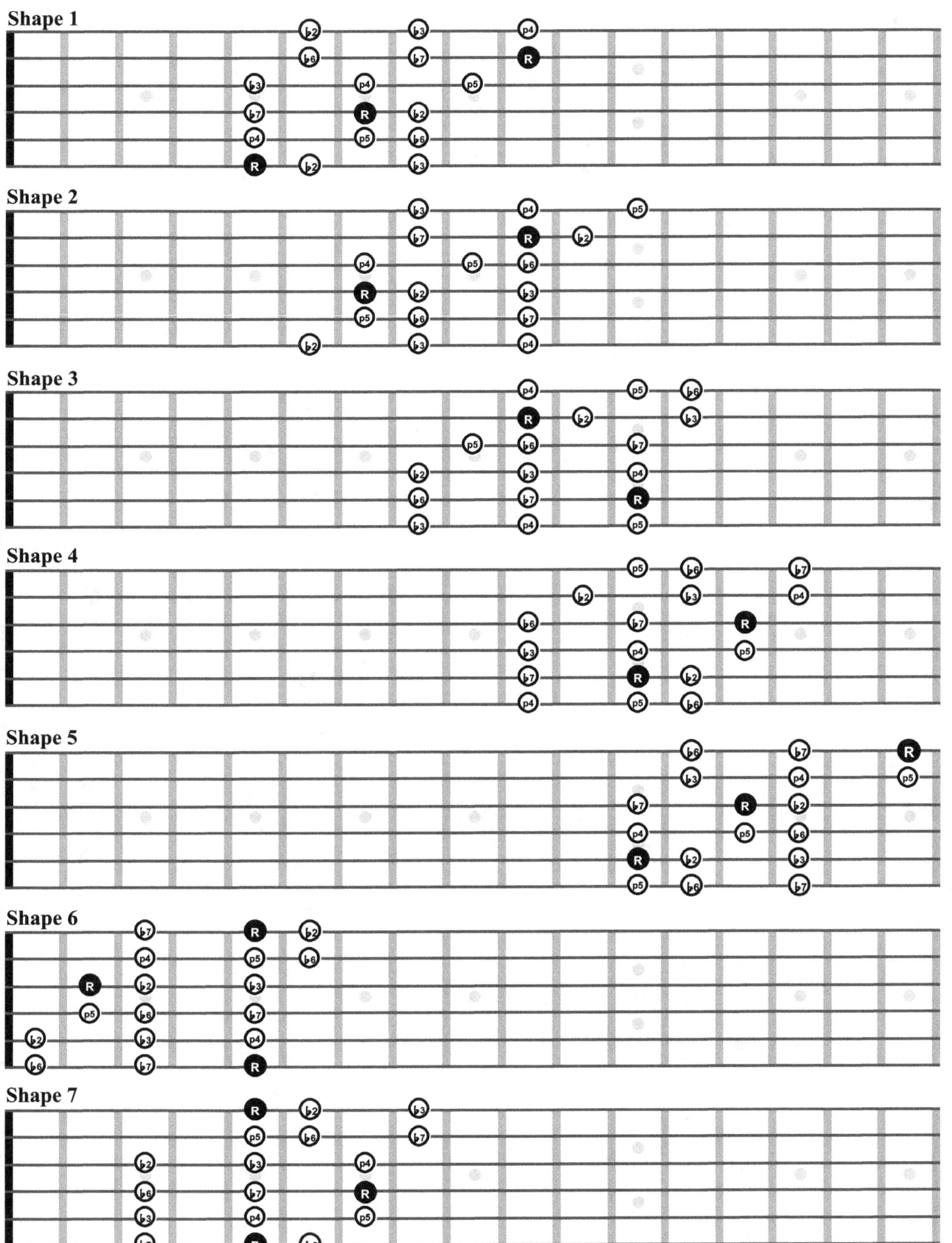

A Lydian Scale

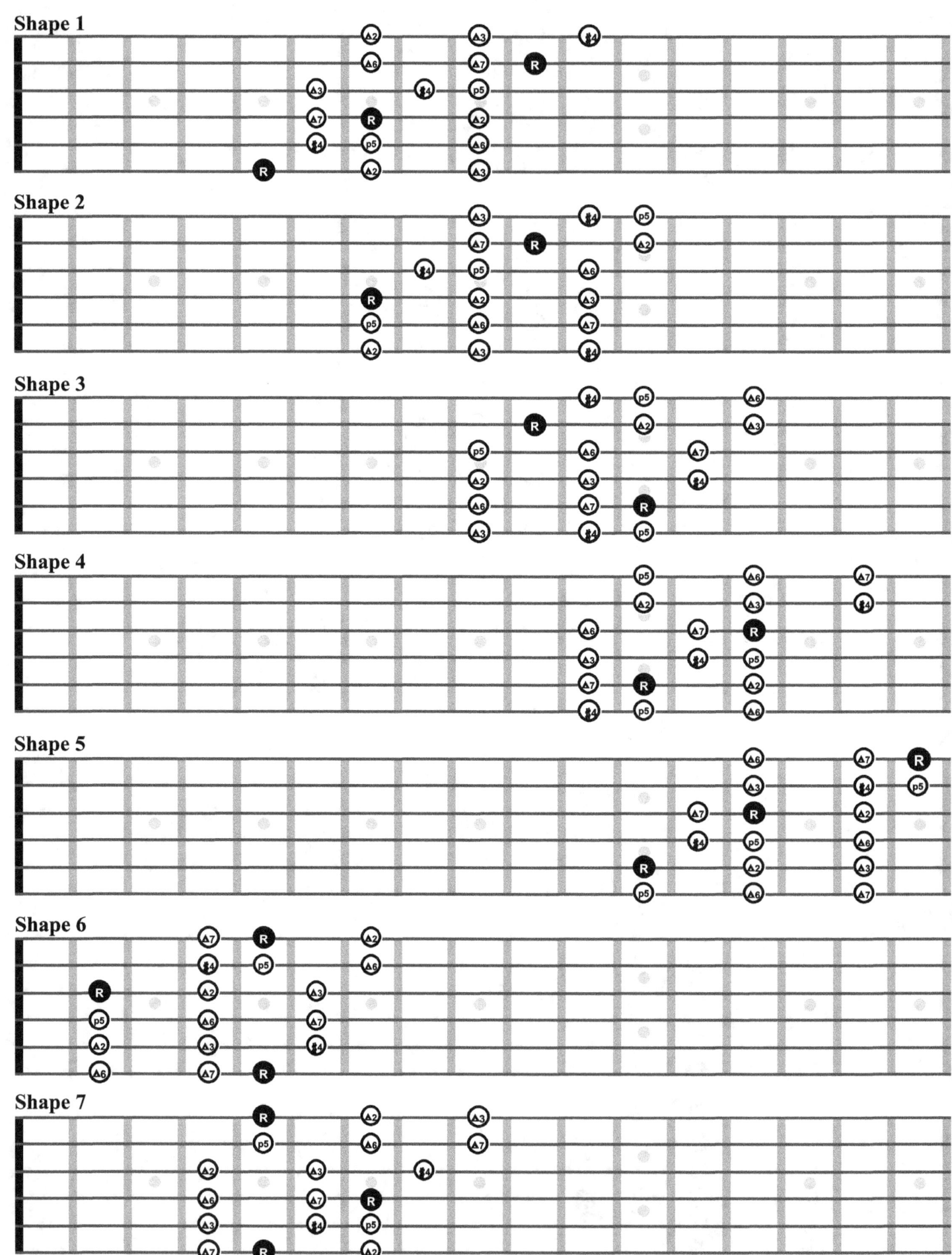

A Mixolydian Scale

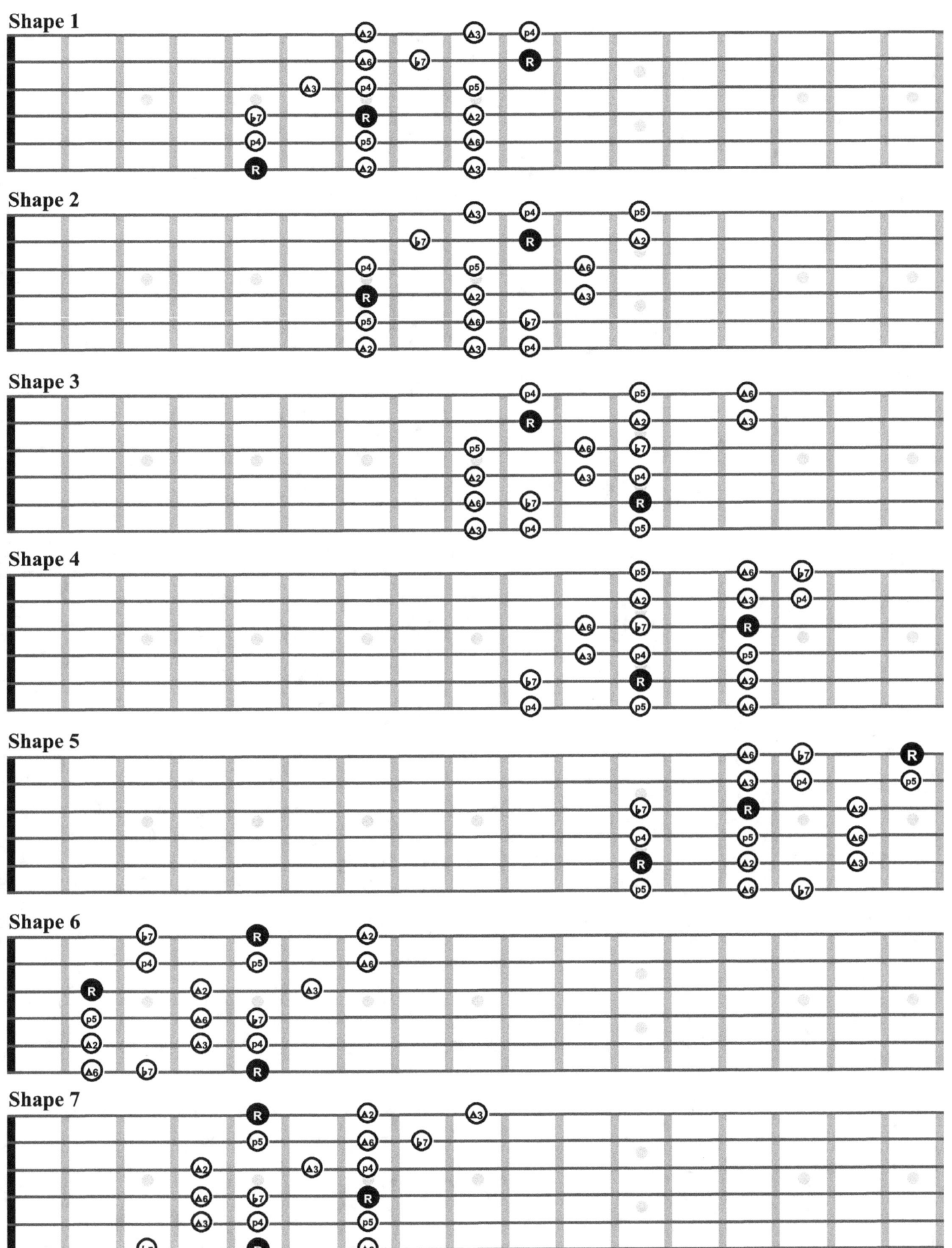

A Aeolian Scale

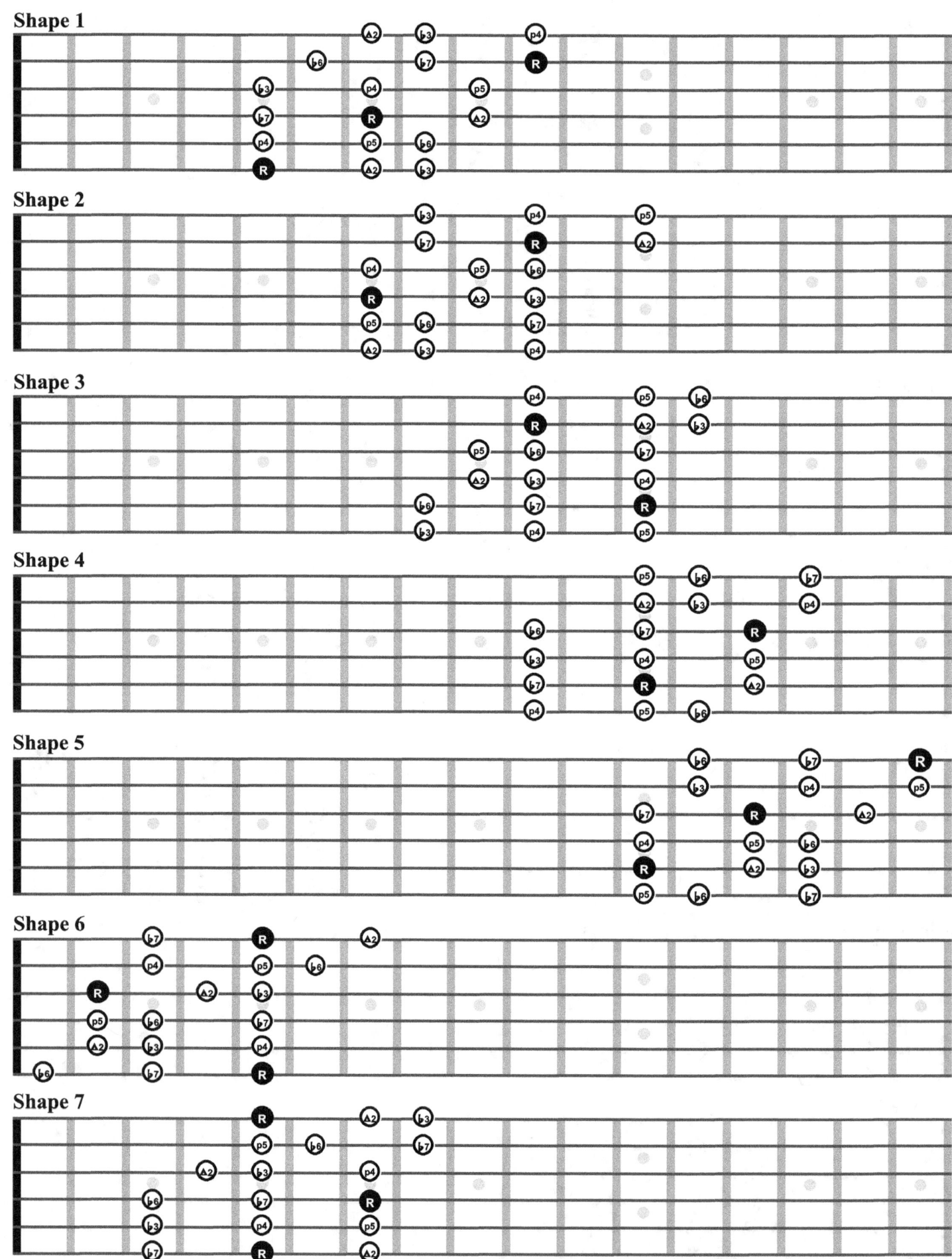

A Locrian Scale

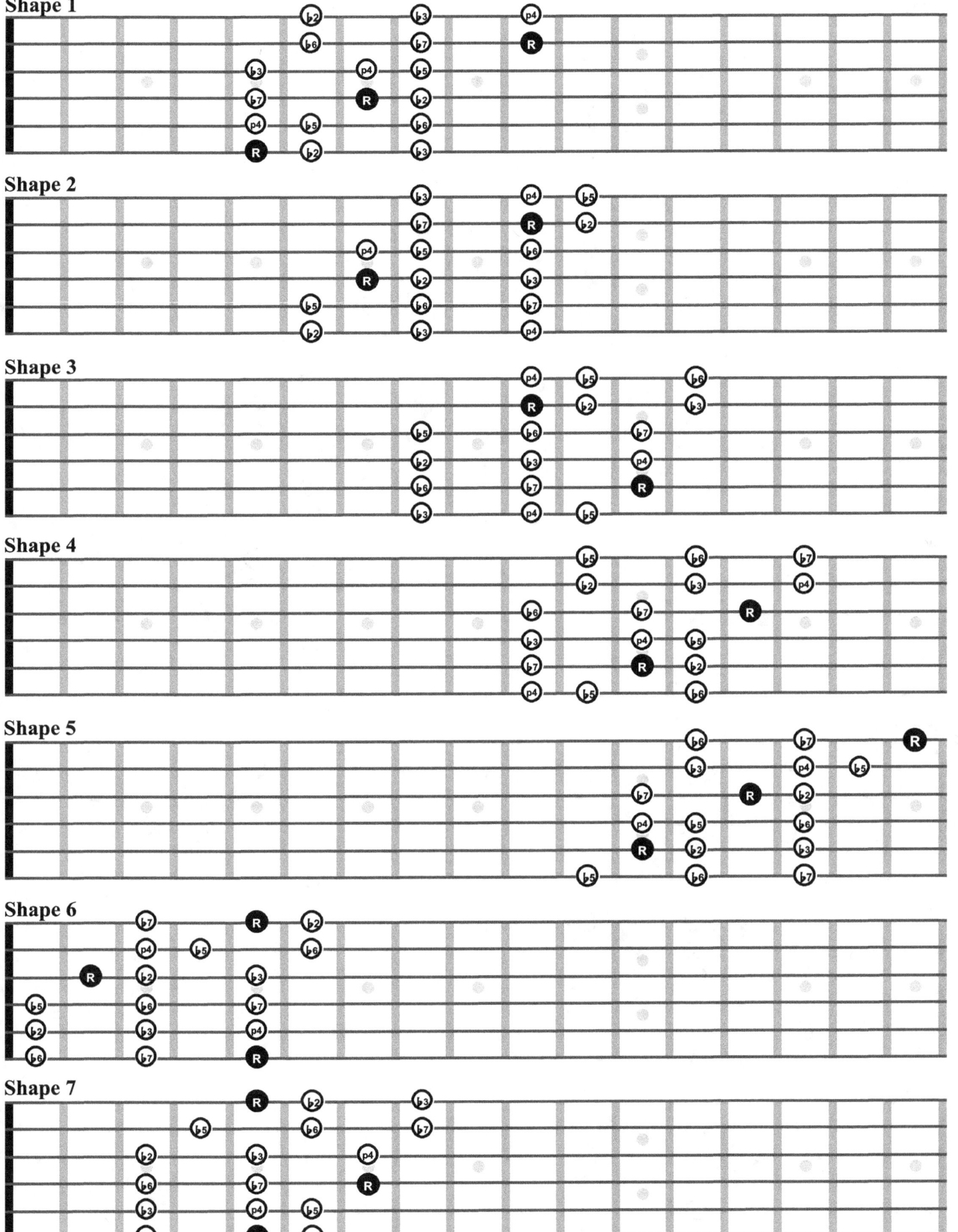

A Harmonic Minor Scale

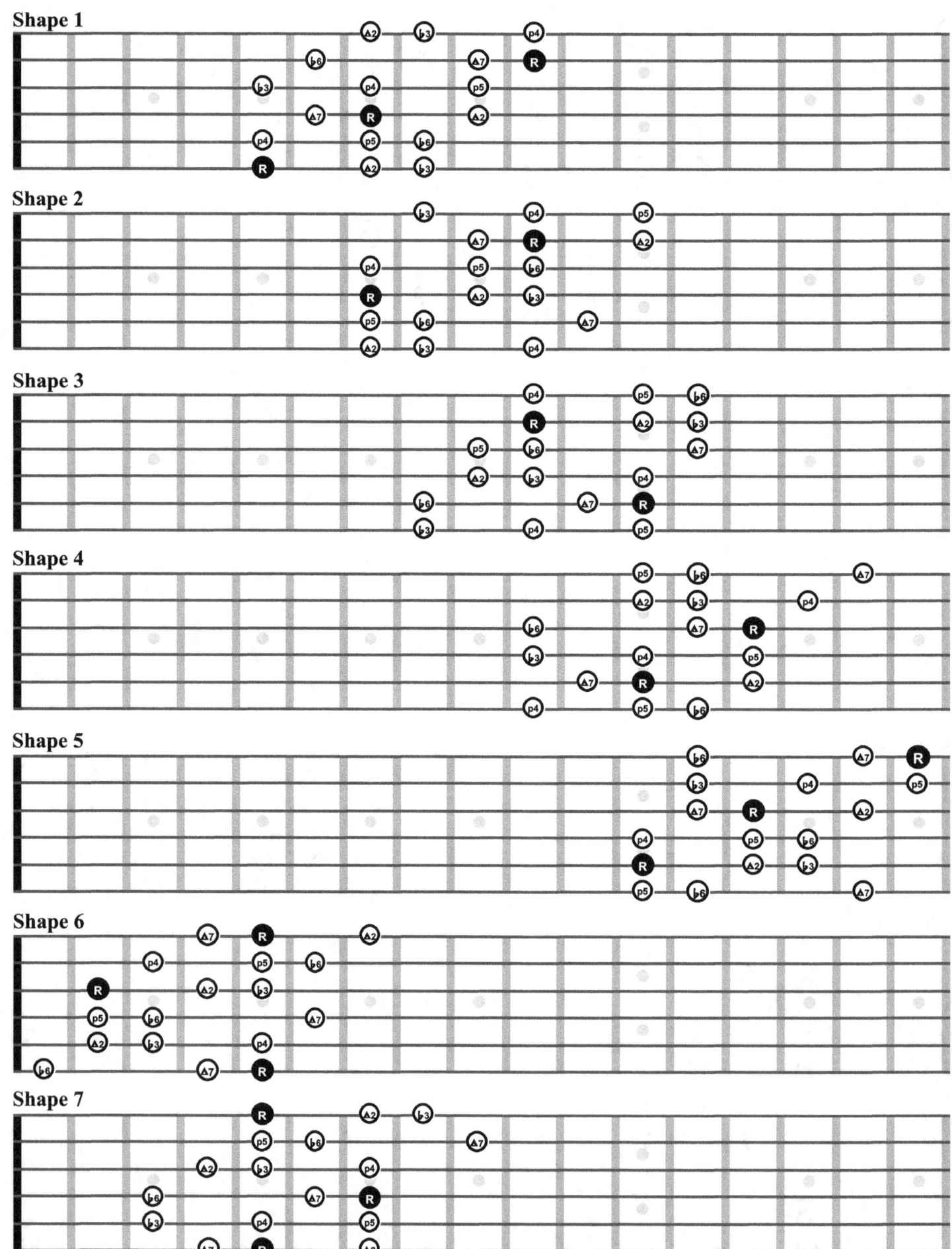

A Locrian #6 Scale

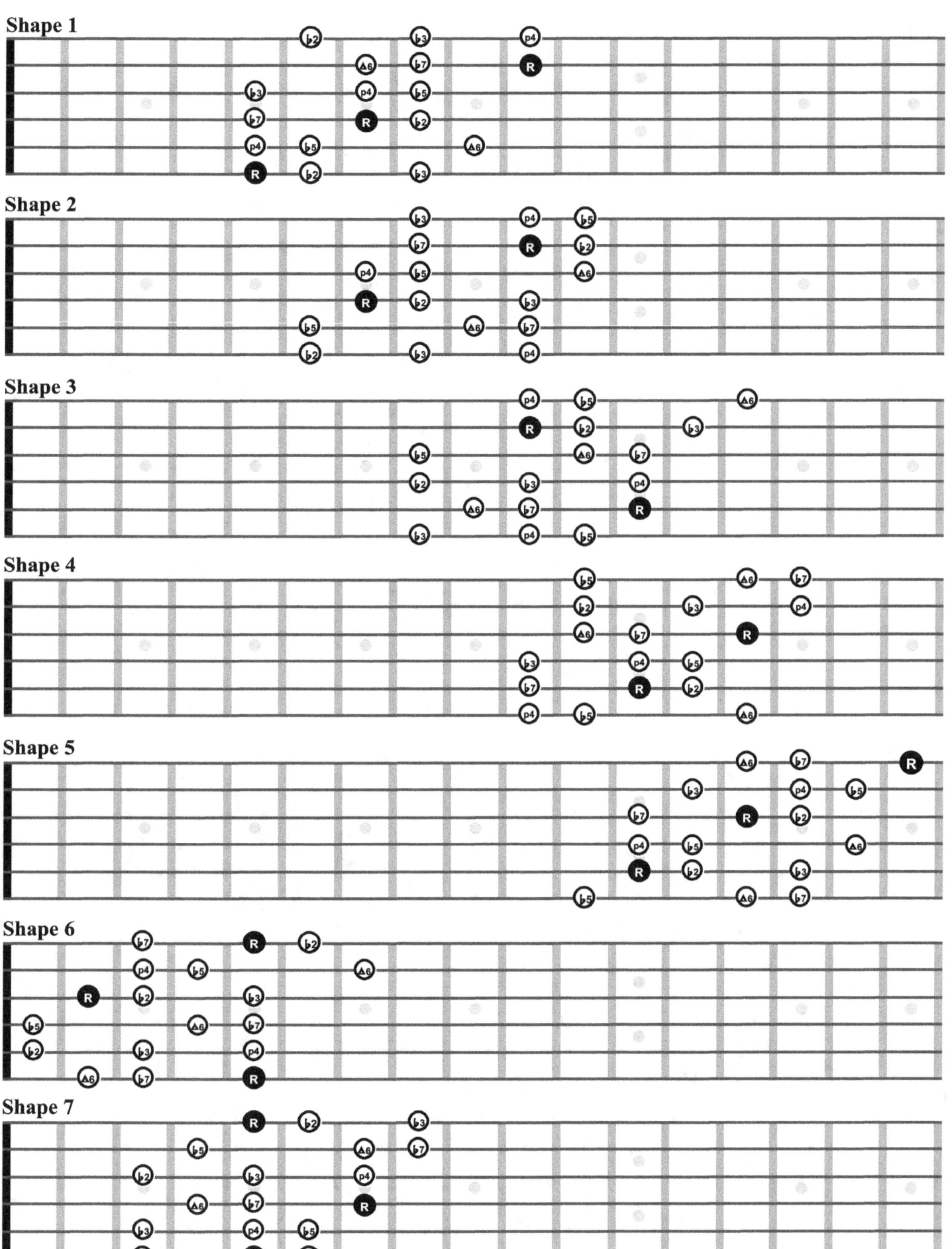

A Ionian Augmented Scale

Shape 1

Shape 2

Shape 3

Shape 4

Shape 5

Shape 6

Shape 7

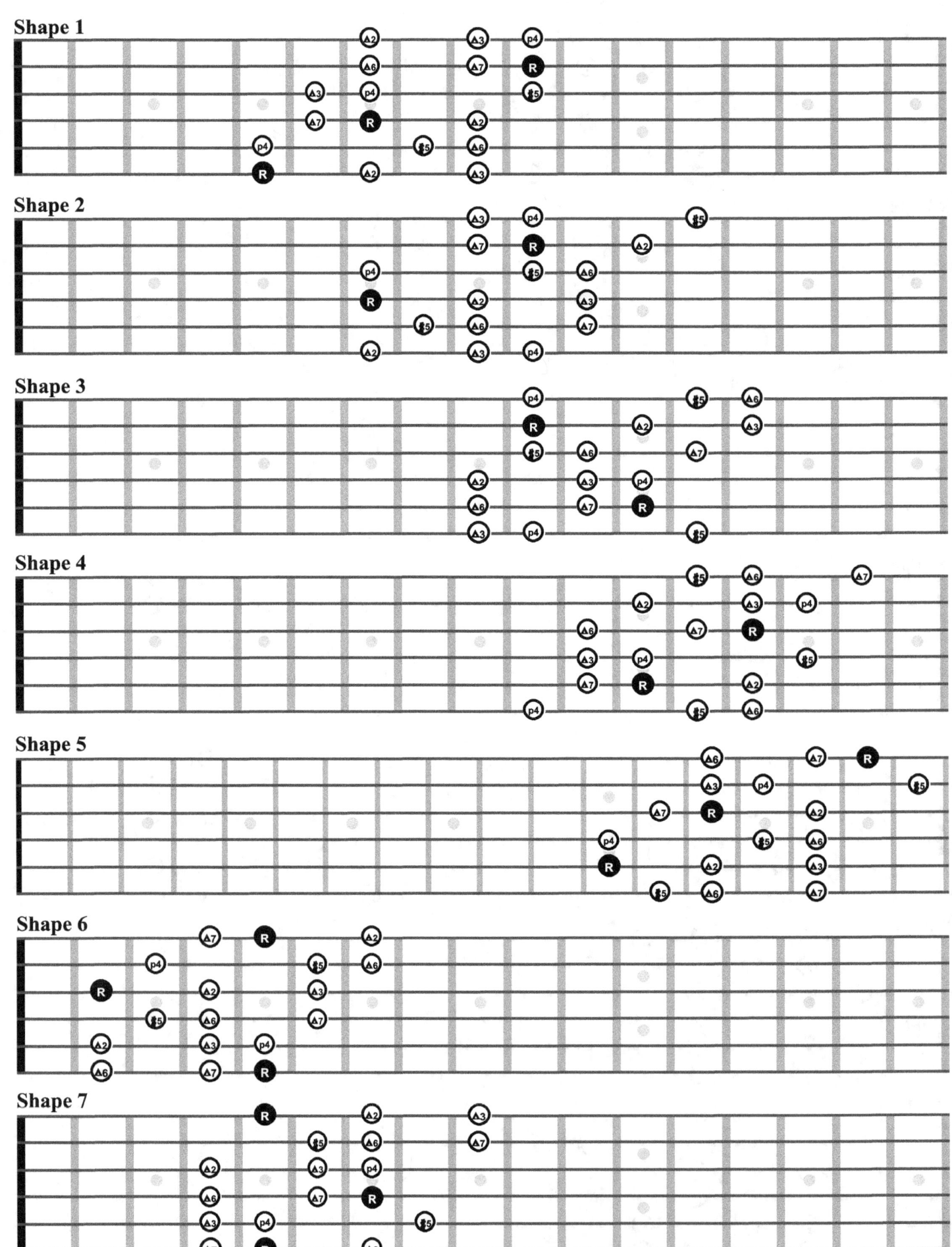

A Dorian #4 Scale

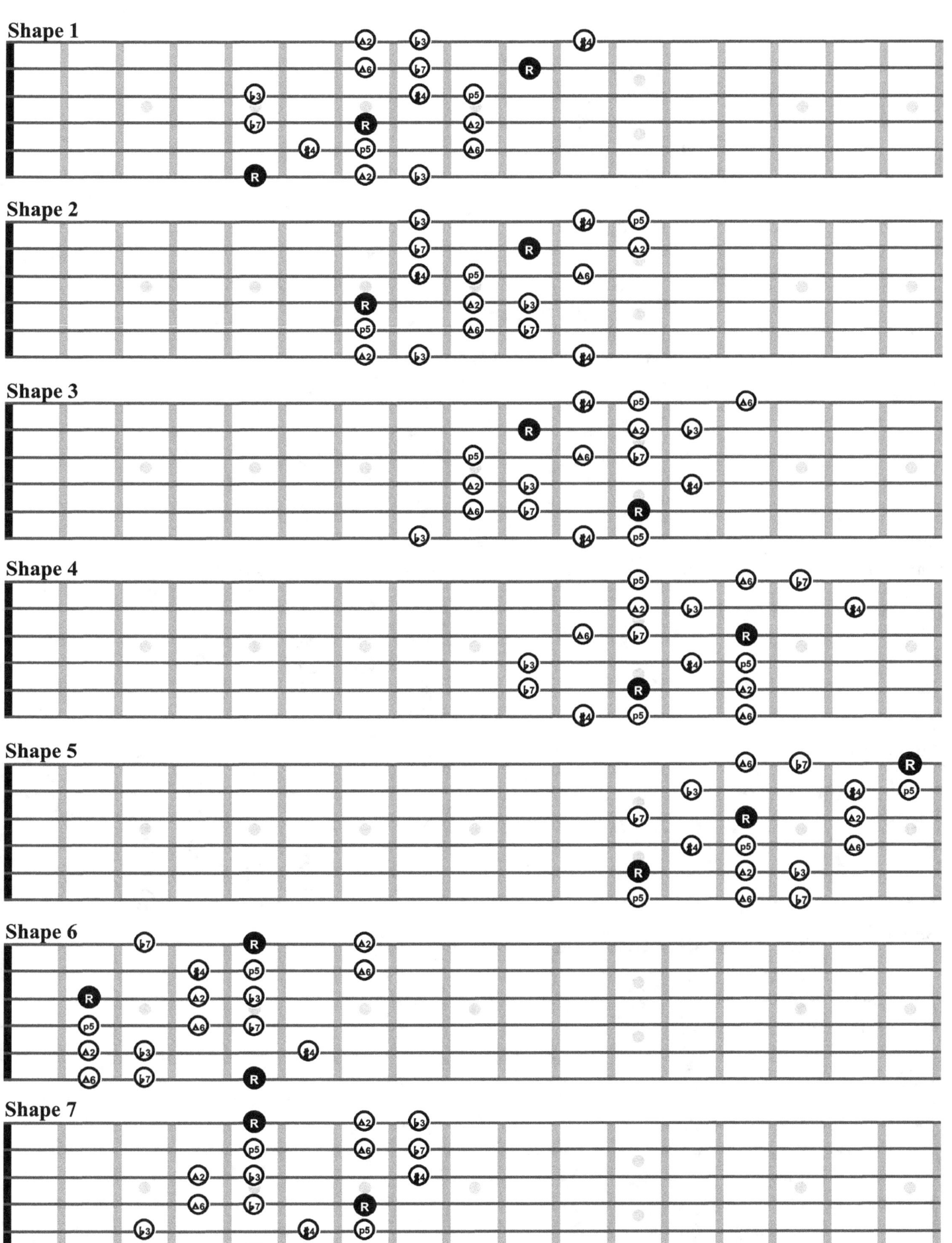

A Phrygian Dominant Scale

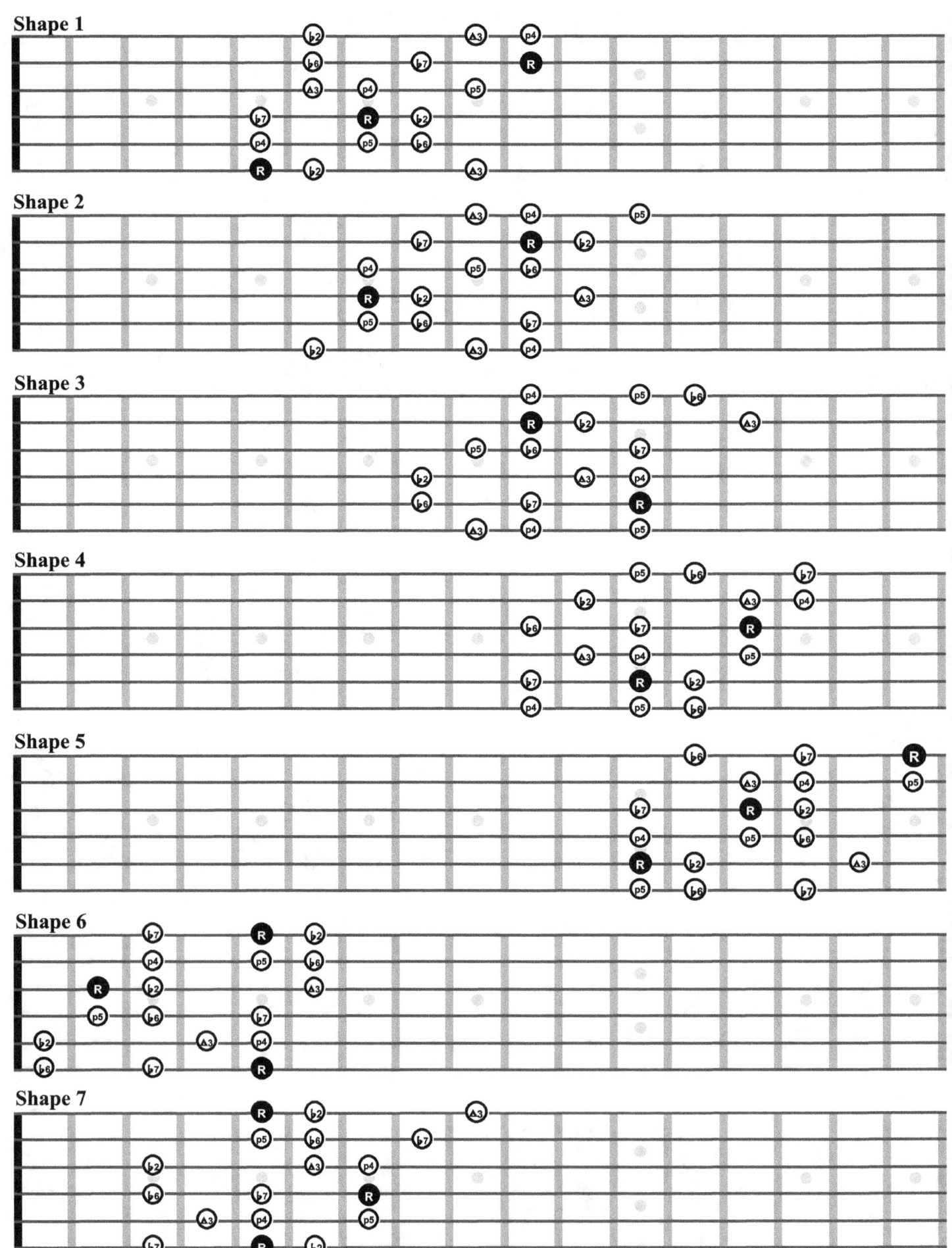

A Lydian #2 Scale

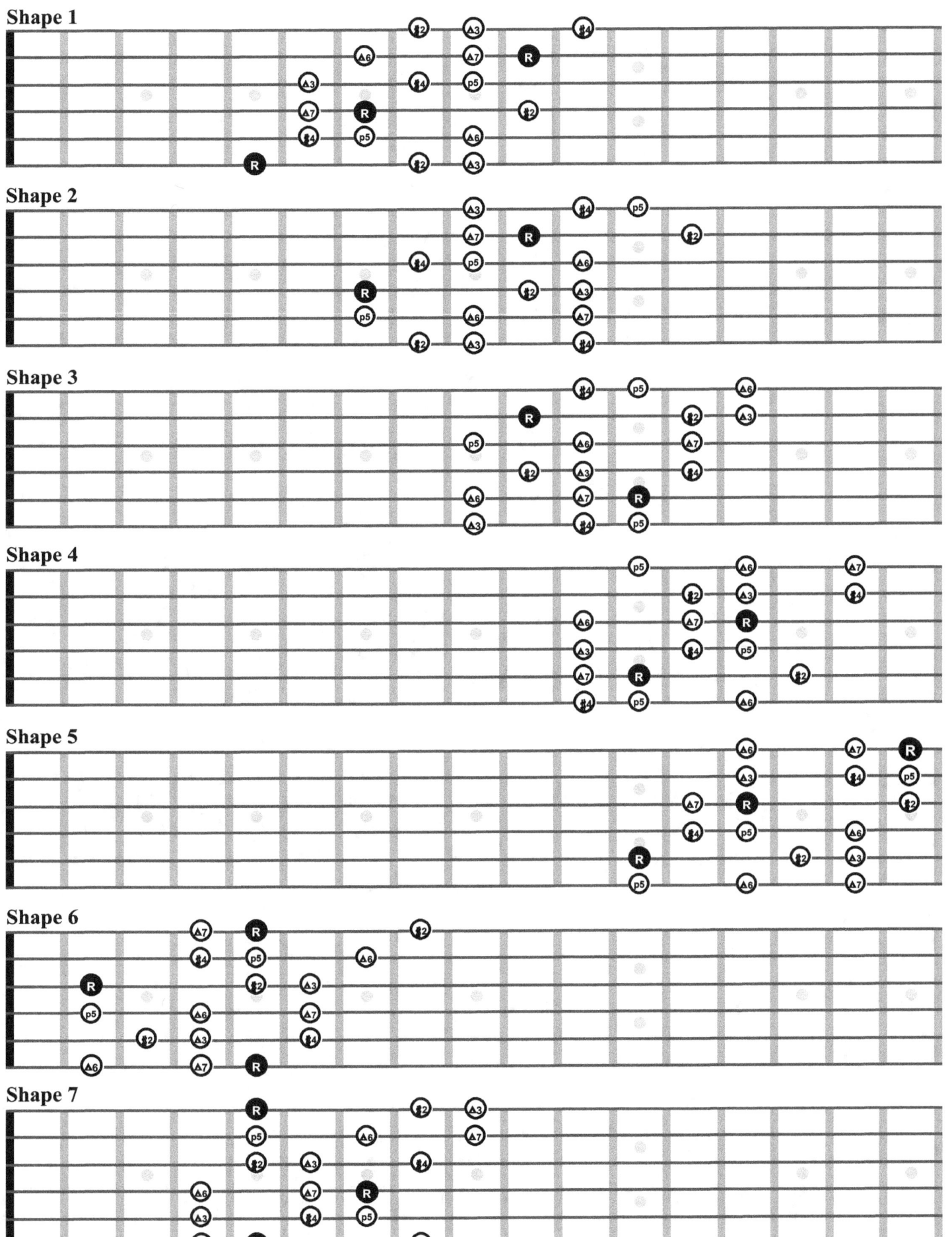

A Ultralocrian Scale

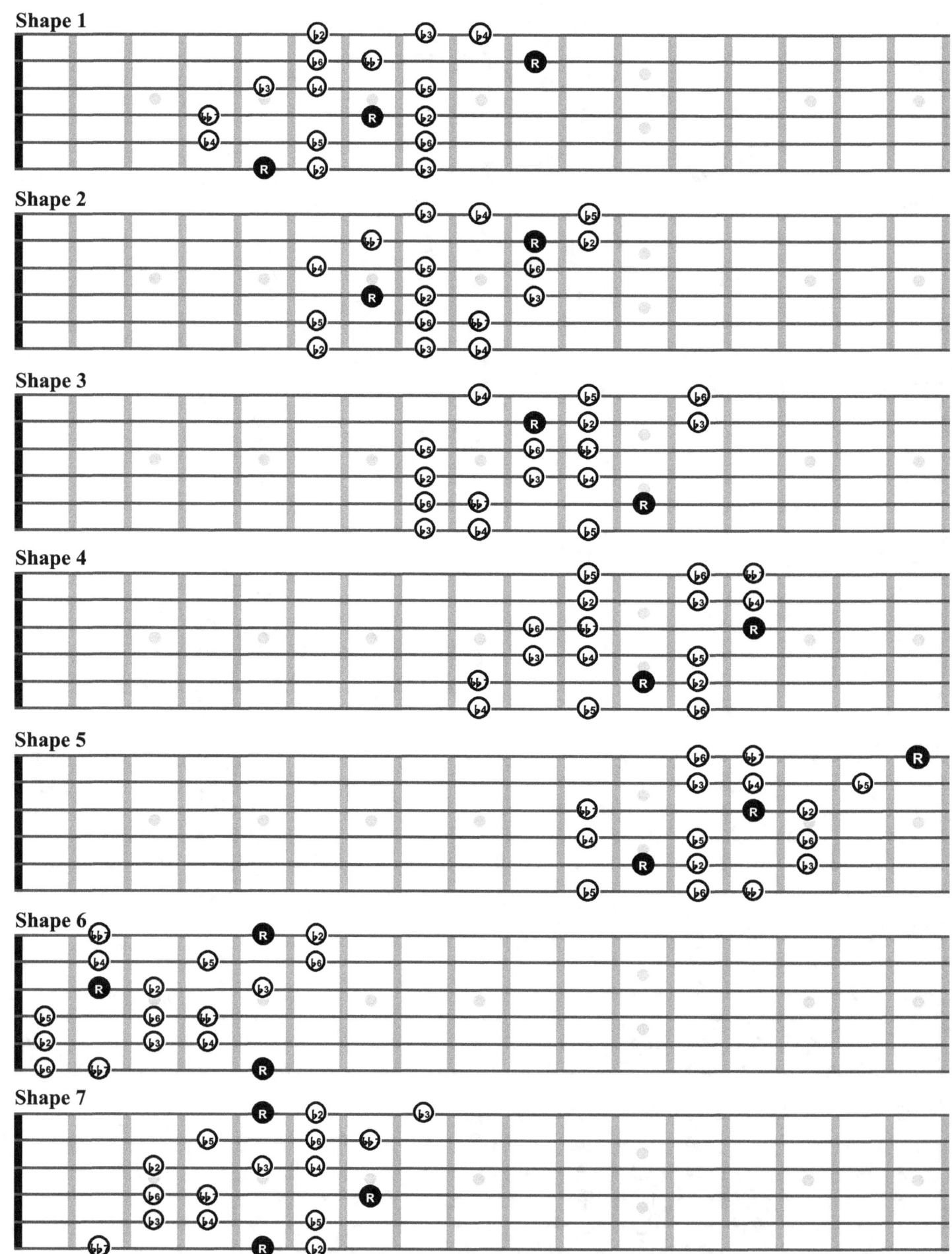

A Melodic Minor Scale

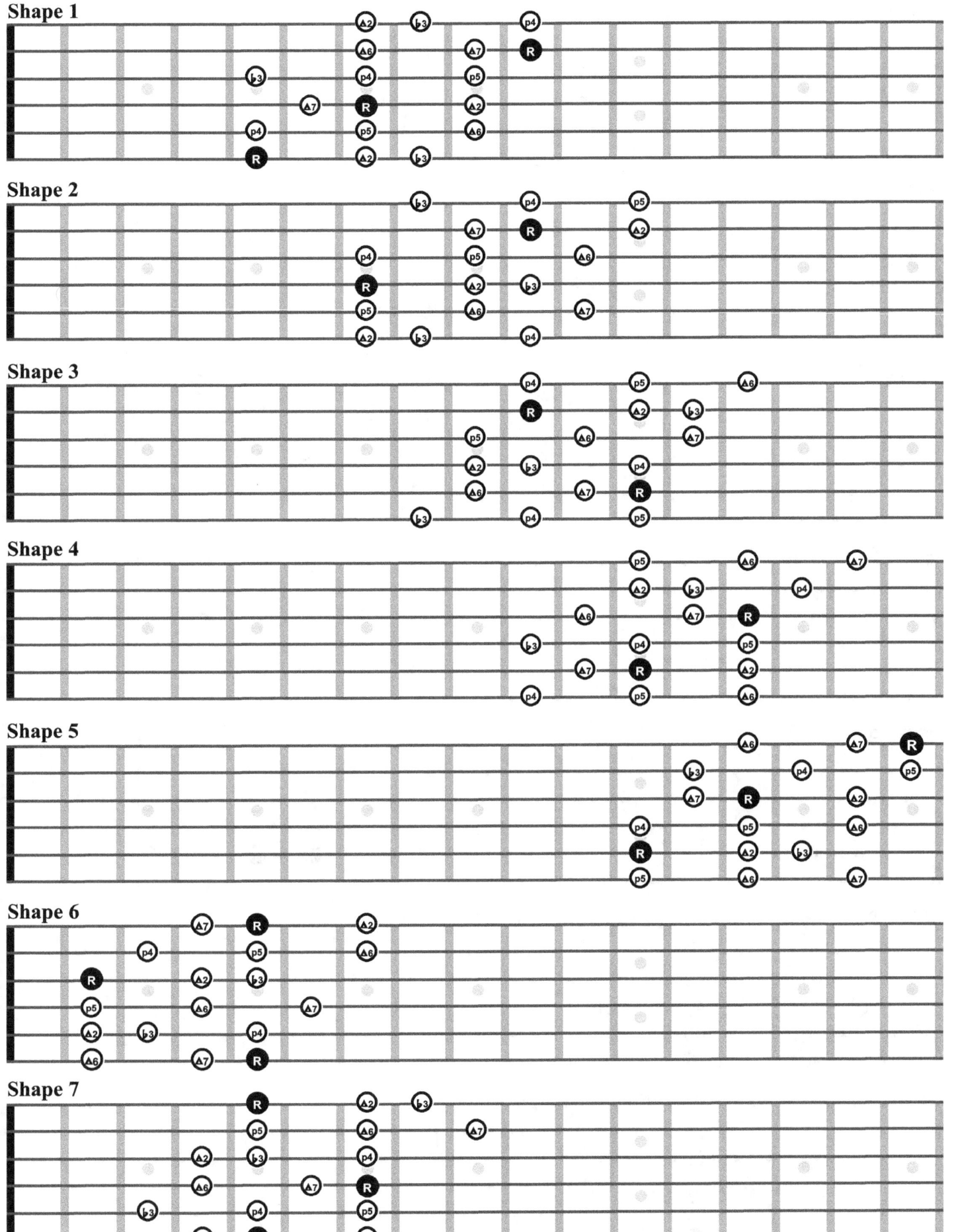

A Dorian b2 Scale

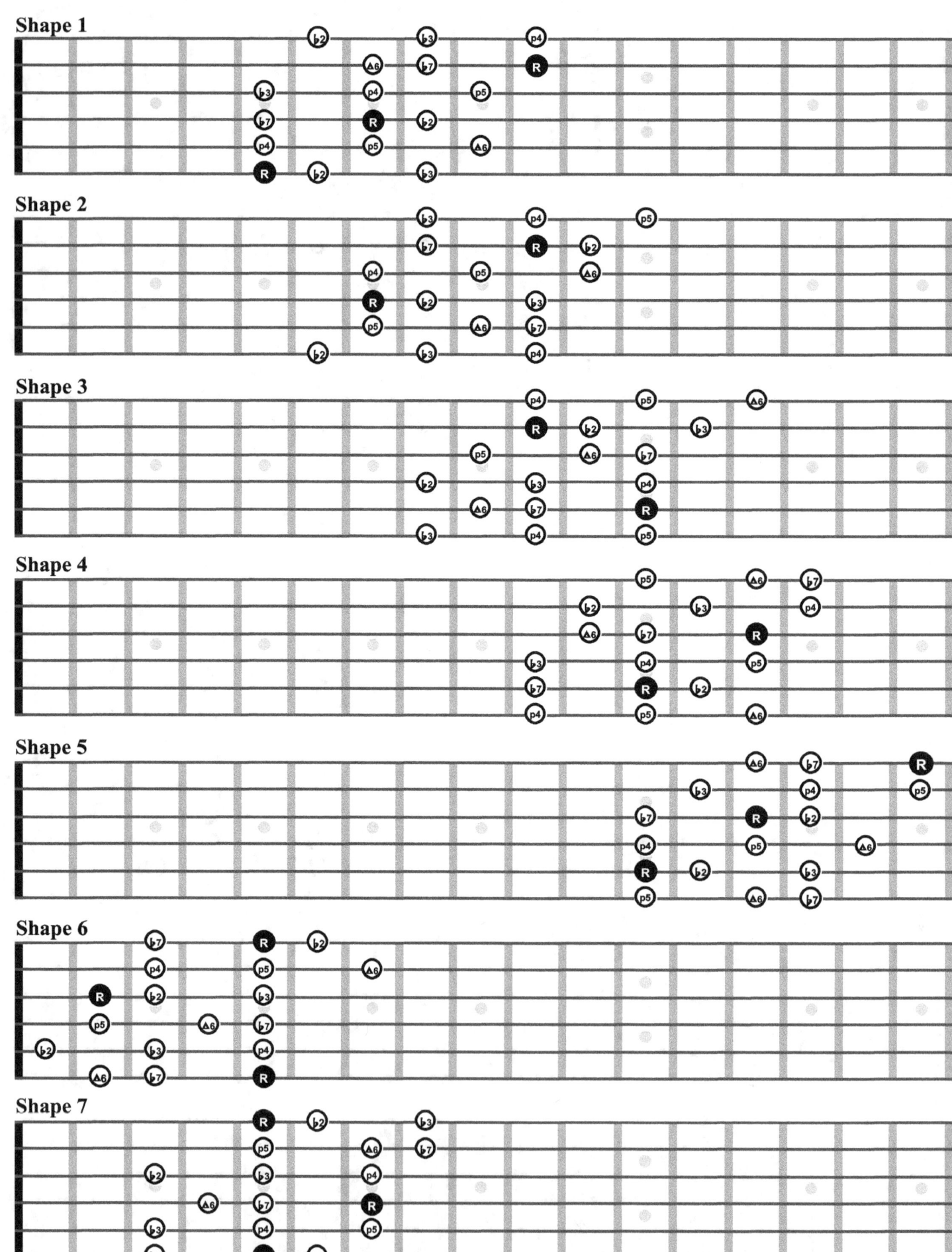

A Lydian Augmented Scale

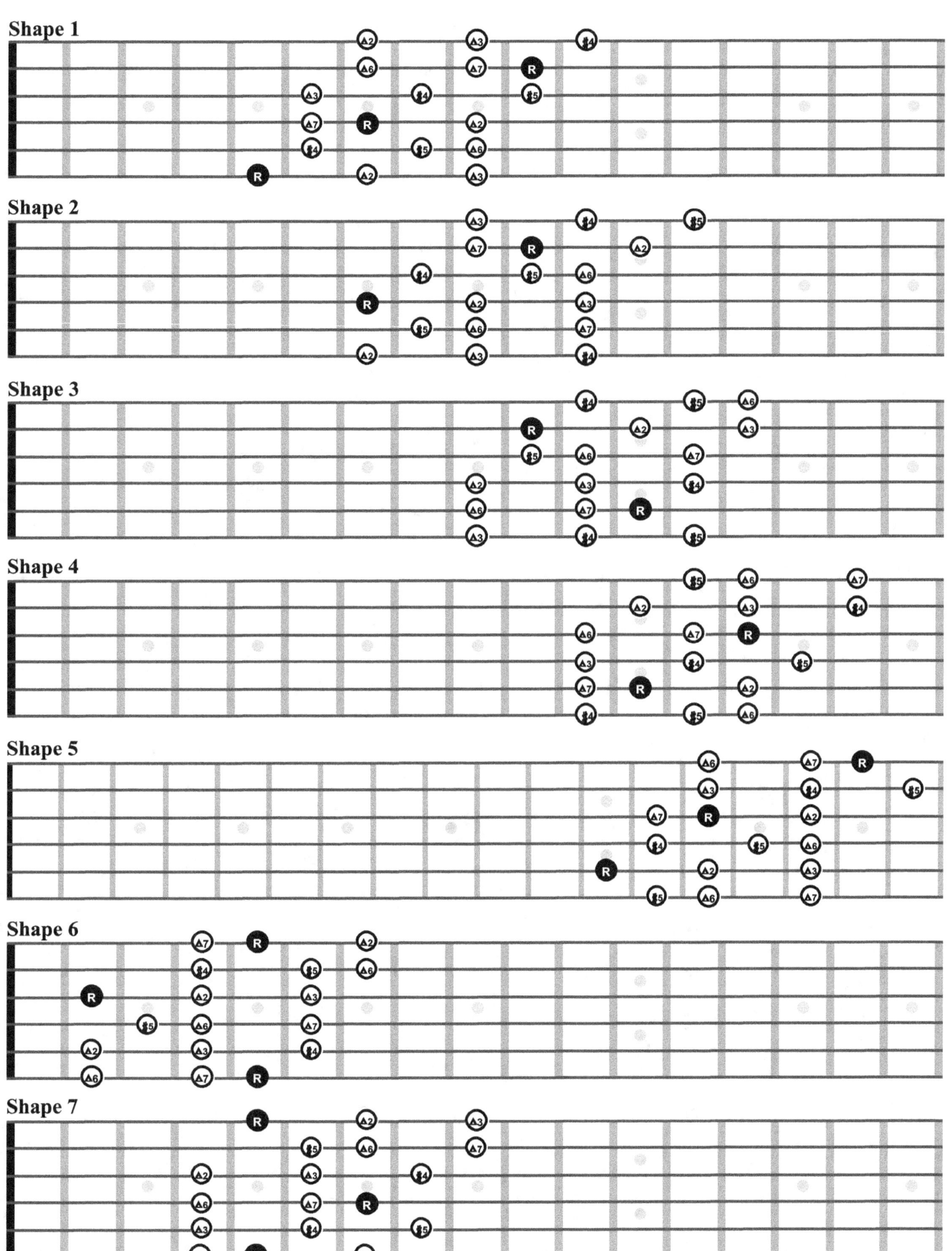

A Lydian Dominant Scale

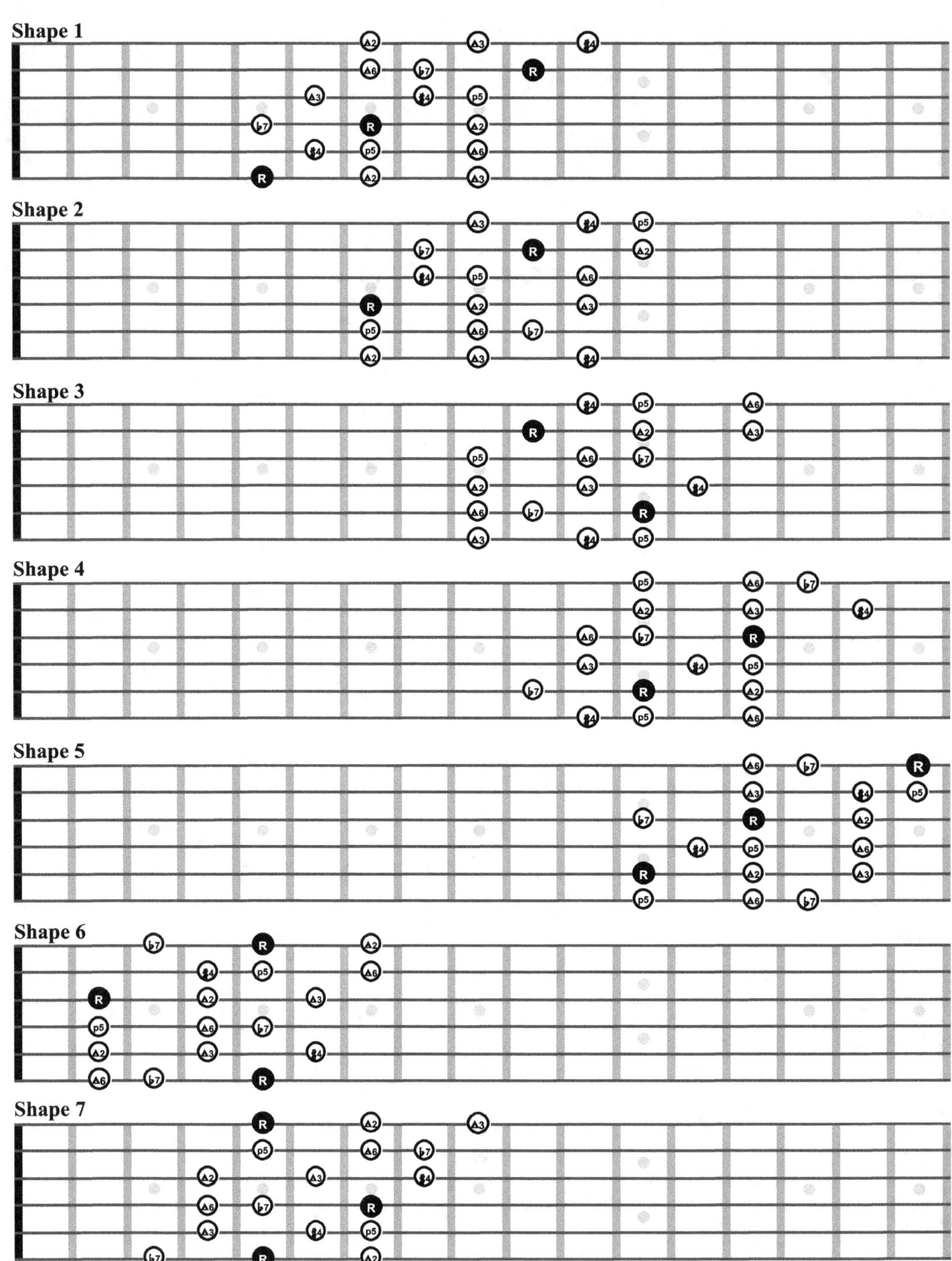

A Mixolydian b6 Scale

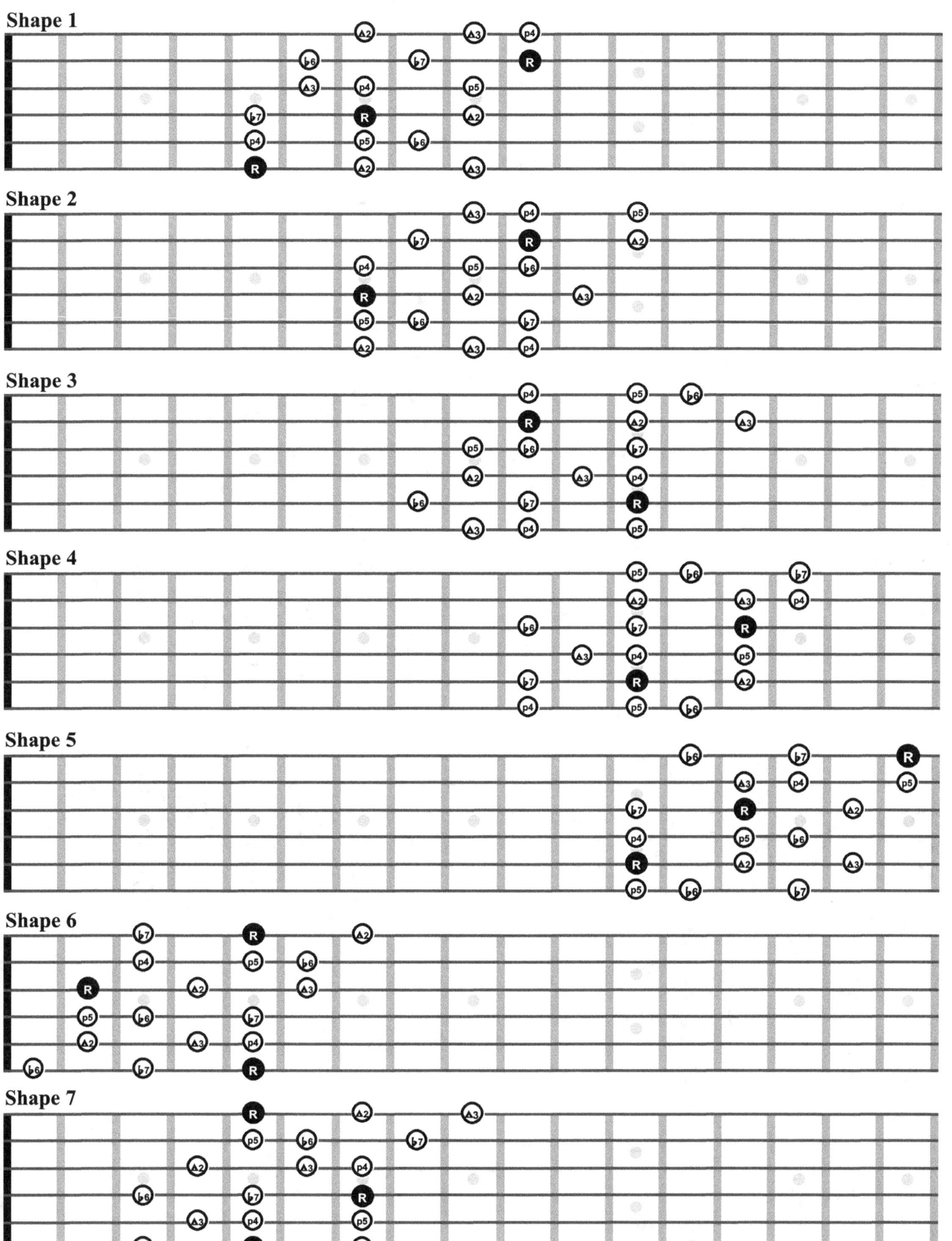

Shape 1

Shape 2

Shape 3

Shape 4

Shape 5

Shape 6

Shape 7

A Locrian #2 Scale

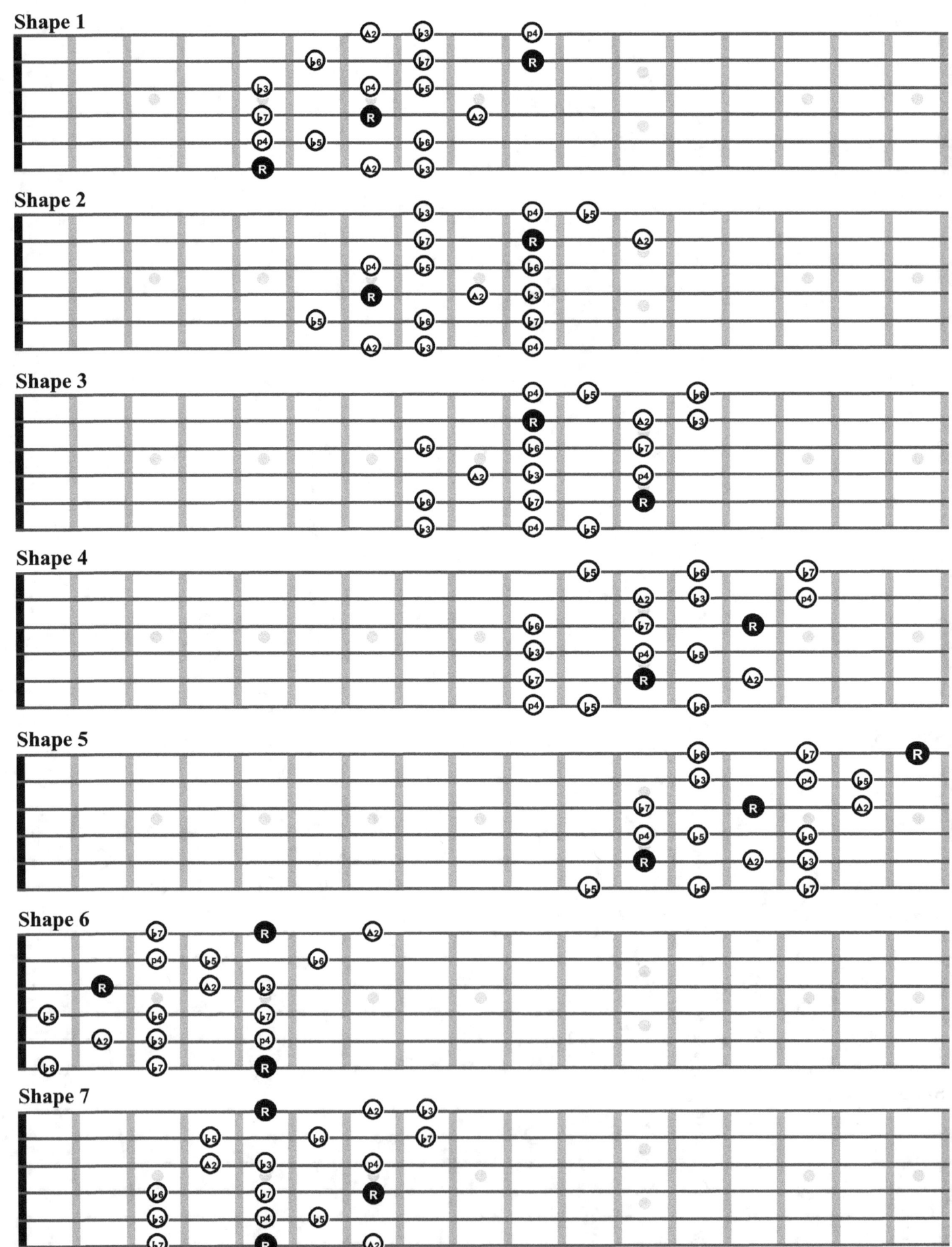

A Altered Scale

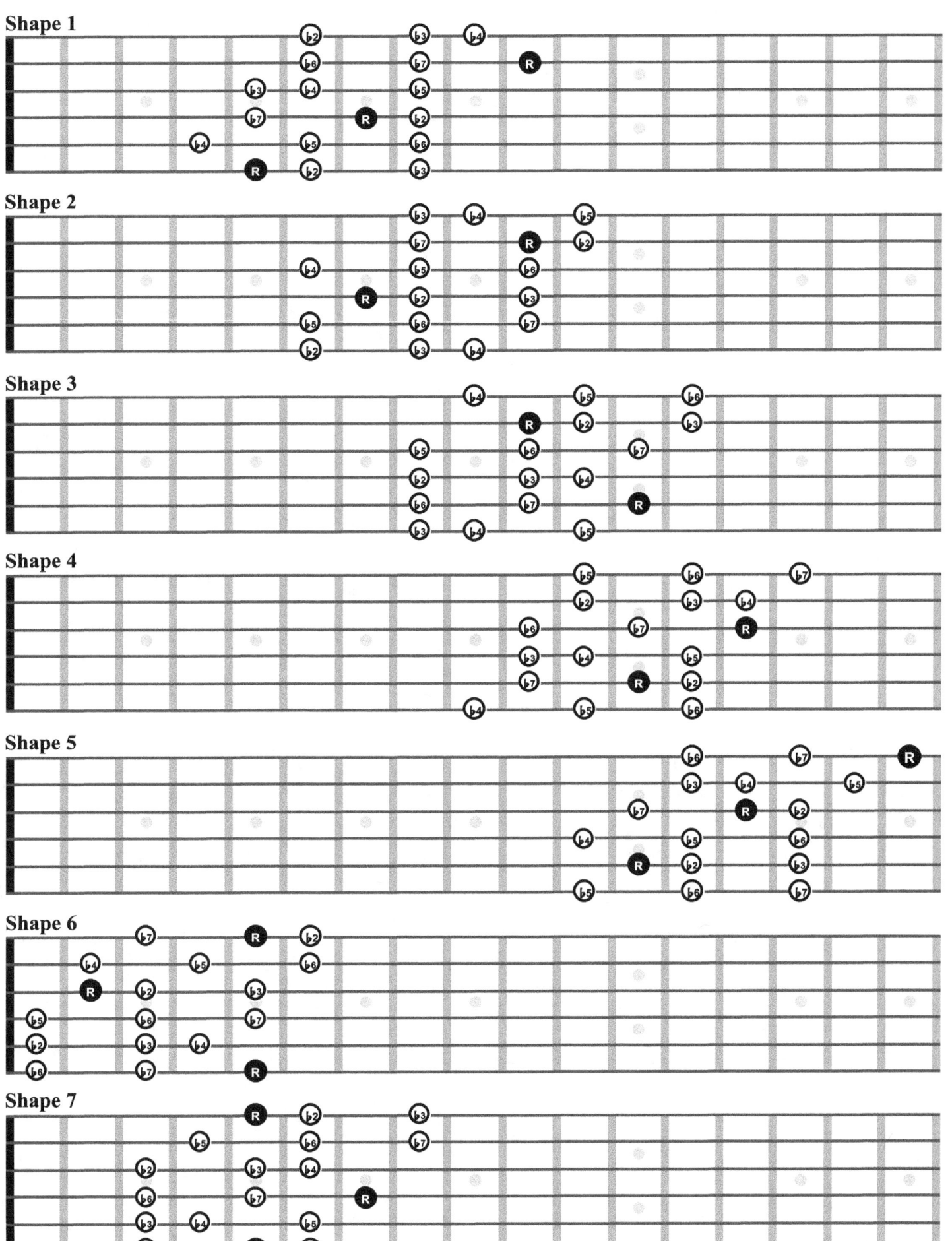